George Leon Walker

Some Aspects of the Religious Life of New England

with special reference to Congregationalists

George Leon Walker

Some Aspects of the Religious Life of New England
with special reference to Congregationalists

ISBN/EAN: 9783337235512

Printed in Europe, USA, Canada, Australia, Japan

Cover: Foto ©Lupo / pixelio.de

More available books at **www.hansebooks.com**

SOME ASPECTS
OF
THE RELIGIOUS LIFE
OF
NEW ENGLAND

WITH

SPECIAL REFERENCE TO CONGREGATIONALISTS.

Lectures

Delivered on the Carew Foundation before Hartford Theological Seminary in 1896.

BY

GEORGE LEON WALKER, D.D.

SILVER, BURDETT AND COMPANY.

New York ... Boston ... Chicago.

1897.

Copyright, 1897,
BY SILVER, BURDETT AND COMPANY.

University Press:
JOHN WILSON AND SON, CAMBRIDGE, U.S.A.

PREFACE.

THE ecclesiastical story of New England has often been told, but with primary reference to its external, institutional, and political aspects. The religious life itself — its dominating motives, its characterizing experiences, its manifestations of spiritual power in the careers of the men and women of the nine generations that have dwelt upon New England soil since the landing of the Pilgrims — has been largely neglected. The writer has long cherished a desire to treat this theme with some degree of fullness, proportionate to what he deems its importance. But the limitations of an engrossing profession, and the disabilities consequent upon ill health, have prevented the accomplishment of his design. Yet the wish has been strong within him; and, being invited by the Trustees of Hartford Theological Seminary to deliver the "Carew Lectures" for 1896, he has made use of the opportunity thus afforded him to present a rapid survey of a field of investigation which he would gladly have traversed in a more leisurely and ample manner, had time and strength permitted him.

HARTFORD, CONN.,
    February 1, 1897.

CONTENTS.

I.
	PAGE
THE PURITAN PERIOD: 1620-1660	7

II.
THE PURITAN DECLINE: 1660-1735 43

III.
THE GREAT AWAKENING AND ITS SEQUELS: 1735-1790 83

IV.
THE EVANGELICAL REAWAKENING: 1790-1859 . 126

V.
THE CURRENT PERIOD: 1859-1896 164

THE RELIGIOUS LIFE OF NEW ENGLAND.

I.

THE PURITAN PERIOD.

THE subject which has been announced for the Carew Course of Lectures this season is: "Some Aspects of the Religious Life of New England, with Special Reference to Congregationalists." It is hoped that the topic, so stated, suggests that what is to be considered is not so much the ecclesiastical story of religious things among our forerunners in these provinces and States, as it is the religious life itself regarded more particularly in its experimental and interior aspects. Of course it will be quite impossible to leave out of view — indeed, to let pass without frequent mention — those ecclesiastical arrangements and semi-political measures which were often the expression, and to some extent also the cause, of the particular qualities of the religious life associated with them. Few communities anywhere have been more distinctly or responsively influenced in the tone and character of their spiritual experiences by social conditions and by legal and ecclesiastical regulations in religious matters than the communities of New England. It is impracticable to ignore or to obscure the agency of these factors in any survey of the more spiritual phenomena which accompanied or, to some degree, flowed from them. But, though not to be ignored, these more external matters are only secondary in the present design, not alone because they have — especially the ecclesiastical side of them — been made, in quite recent times and by several writers, the subject of a consideration so minute and painstaking as might well incline one to hesitate to traverse ground so carefully surveyed already; but chiefly because these things, in themselves considered, save so far as they affect or illustrate the deeper things of the spiritual life itself, are aside from the immediate purpose of these lectures.

That purpose is to set forth, if it may be, in some degree of clearness, the men and women of different periods of New England story in a way to enable us to see what they thought, and especially what they felt, about those great problems of religious experience which, in one form or another, and with varying degrees of intensity of interest, press upon every generation of our race. For it is this, more than any matter of outward condition or ecclesiastical form, which is the truest bond of fellowship and acquaintance between times and men. If we can understand even a little better than we do the real religious life of our fathers and mothers of two, four, six, and eight generations ago, we shall not only have gained some distinct accession of knowledge concerning them, but they will become more the objects of a living interest and of some degree at least of sympathy, as being in their time and way concerned about questions of as vital importance to ourselves as to them, and of real, however sometimes disregarded, importance to all.

With this preliminary statement respecting the general object proposed in the lectures which are to follow, the topic suggested for consideration on this particular occasion is the Religious Life of New England in the First or the Planting Period of our History. The period in question may be roughly estimated as from 1620, the time of the arrival at Plymouth of the Pilgrim settlers, to about 1655 or 1660, — a period substantially covering the lives, or at least the active lives, of the first settlers of all the early New England colonies.

One general fact which confronts us on the threshold of any inquiry into the qualities of the religious life of the first generation or two of New England's progenitors is, that that life was essentially a transplantation into, and not a new product of, this American soil. The founders of the New England colonies did not intend — to use a somewhat hackneyed current phrase — to institute any "new departure," religiously speaking, in coming hither. The motive which brought them here was not, strictly speaking, one essentially belonging to the religious life. So far as appears, all the substantial qualities and experiences of that life could have been manifested and enjoyed — nay, for years had been conspicuously manifested and enjoyed — under social and ecclesiastical conditions from which nevertheless they felt compelled, for other reasons than purely religious ones, to come out. The fathers did, indeed, inaugurate a new departure here of wide and far-reaching significance. In its remoter consequences religion has doubtless been deeply affected by it. But religion was not what they intended to modify, — only the ecclesiastical setting of religion. The issue on which they, Pilgrims and Puritans alike, left the sweet fields and comfortable homes and settled ways of the land of their birth for this raw wilderness, was primarily an issue of the politics rather than of the substance of the religious life.

To understand the quality of that life, therefore, as the New England fathers and mothers felt it, thought of it, and illustrated it, we cannot hastily pick them up, standing on this fresh soil of America and gathered in the little communities of Plymouth, the Bay, Connecticut, New Haven, or Rhode Island colonies; but we must take a glance at them in their English home, see something of the spiritual causes which made them what they were, the views of religious truth they held to be fundamental, the inward experiences they deemed necessary and which had wrought out in them the type of a religious life which they simply brought with them over here, with no desire of changing it, and with no expectation that anything they were doing ever would change it for them or for their posterity.

The great English movement of the hundred years previous to the advent of the Pilgrim and Puritan fathers to these shores, which we call the Reformation in England, was all along closely connected with, and sometimes dominated by, political considerations. This, which was in a measure true of the Reformation movement on the Continent among the French and German speaking nations, was in a still more emphatic manner the case on British soil. In England the questions of national independence and the separation of the government from foreign ecclesiastical control oftentimes and for long periods occupied the attention of men, to the comparative obscuration of questions of a more purely religious character. Men of the most opposite views of ecclesiastical polity, and the most contrary types of religious belief and behavior, united with one another all through the later days of Henry VIII. and most of those of Elizabeth, in supporting English supremacy in Church and State as against the claims of the Papacy; and it was only as dominating anxiety about the political situation gradually declined, through the growing recognition of the fact that the national victory had been secured, that the differences between reformers themselves on ecclesiastical and religious questions became prominent.

Not, indeed, but that through the whole period in question there was beneath all outward manifestations what might be called an undercurrent of somewhat steadily growing religious life. Ever since the days of Wycliffe, — in fact, for nearly two centuries before the time we are speaking of, — a leaven had been working in English life which witnessed in every generation to the possession by some, and in the aggregate doubtless by a great many, of a really spiritual conception of religious truth and the life which should flow from it. Especially in the East of England, and among plain people of farms and hamlets, this early sown seed of reformation-grain bore real, though stunted, harvest. The Scriptures in Wycliffe's and Tyndale's translations had brought the truths of the Gospel to the acquaintance of many and to the loving acceptance of not a few, who were thus preparing the way for a fuller light and a more vigorous religious life whenever opportunity for it should arise.

But the great national revolt which successfully asserted England's independency alike in civil and ecclesiastical affairs, however prompted by political considerations mainly, could not be without speedy and profound spiritual consequences to English religion. For years before the time when, with the destruction of the Spanish Armada, in 1588, the last reasonable hope of ever reducing England again to Papal control was finally extinguished, the Church of that country found itself in possession of articles of religious belief wherein the whole momentous transition from a sacerdotal system in which, as in that of Rome, responsibility for a man's religious life and salvation is practically taken off him and laid upon a corporate institution called the Church,

ENGLISH RELIGIOUS ANTECEDENTS. 13

to a view of things, on the contrary, which lays that responsibility upon the man himself, is plainly indicated and expressed. No change more momentous to the religious life can be imagined than that. And it was one by which for more than two generations previous to the coming of the New England planters to our soil, all classes alike of Protestant English people — save during the brief and reactionary reign of Mary Tudor — found themselves influenced and well-nigh dominated. Religion had become a personal, not a corporate, matter.

Puritans, who felt bound, in spite of corruptions they still discerned in a State Church, to adhere to a national Establishment, and Separatists, who felt constrained to withdraw from such an Establishment, were at one in their common recognition and experience of the profound effect on every serious-minded man of the Protestant principle of personal responsibility in religious matters. Thought was turned inward upon self, instead of outward upon ceremonies. Relieved of the artificial burden of an official system which put a successive range of barriers — confessions, penances, absolutions, masses, sacraments — between the soul and its Maker, the actual burden of sin and accountableness, of duty and danger, came more and more to be an individually recognized and powerfully felt factor in the spiritual experience.

This altered quality of English religious life, which naturally grew out of the change from Romanism to Protestantism, was strengthened, for the immediate predecessors of the immigrants to this country and for themselves, by the peculiar character of the religious instruction, which now for about fifty years had been increasingly prominent in the pulpits and in some of the university chairs of England.

Whether the Thirty-nine Articles of the English Church, ratified in 1563, and which were essentially the same as the forty-two Articles of the Edwardean episode of ten years previous, are or are not susceptible of an Arminian interpretation has been an oftentime debated question. But there can be no question that speedily after their ratification by royal authority a very marked intensification of Calvinistic opinions began to characterize the most influential preaching and teaching of English pulpits and lecture-rooms. A main cause of this change was the return to England of a considerable body of able and learned men who had been exiled during the terrible five years of the Marian period between Edward and Elizabeth. These men had in their expatriation, at Zurich, Geneva, Frankfort, and Basel, been received with hospitality by the Continental reformers, and had come, many of them, to sympathize not only with the practices in church usage, but with the doctrinal opinions which prevalently characterized the theologians of Southwestern Germany and Switzerland. Men like the two brothers Pilkington, successively Masters of St. John's College at Cambridge, and Roger Kelke, Master of Magdalen, brought back with them not only a spirit of opposition to "ceremonies" as pronounced almost

INFLUENCE OF CALVINISM.

as that of any Separatist, but a Calvinism as austere as Calvin's.

But the most potent influence which molded the preaching of the generation of religious instructors with whom our Pilgrim and Puritan ancestors were most closely associated, and which had therefore most agency in molding the type of their religious experience, emanated probably from two quite different men;— one, the occupant of a professor's chair at Cambridge, where, as Lady Margaret Professor of Divinity, Thomas Cartwright taught both the polity and doctrine of Geneva, profoundly influencing the younger and rising class of university men; the other, an impassioned, physically deformed, but logical, powerful, and spiritual preacher in the same university, William Perkins, whose strenuous, searching, and ultra-Calvinistic discourses left such ineffaceable impressions on several of our ablest New England ministers of the first generation that they have been made the subject of distinct biographic record. And even where, as in the case of Dr. Whitgift,— successively Lady Margaret and Regius Professor of Divinity, Master of Trinity, and Vice-Chancellor of Cambridge University,— no sympathy with non-conformity was found, there was often a high degree of accordancy with the Continental divines of the high-Calvinist type in matters of theology. It was in 1595 that what are known as the Lambeth Articles — so called from the place of their subscription at the palace of that name in London, and beyond comparison the most vigorous symbol of Calvinism ever framed as an expression of English-speaking faith — were approved by no less a representative of the whole English Church than Archbishop Whitgift himself, then elevated to the See of Canterbury.

The prevailing type of doctrine, therefore, in all Puritan as well as in Separatist circles was strenuously, not to say severely, Calvinistic. John Robinson, reckoned in many ways a liberal and tolerant man and preacher, was in 1619, at his place of exile in Holland, put forth as the defender of the decrees of the Synod of Dort, then just promulgated, against animadversions upon them by Episcopius, the distinguished Arminian Leyden professor.

Already, years before they came here, the chief pastors of these New England churches — Cotton, Hooker, Shepherd, Mather — had been known as pronounced, not to say extreme, Calvinists. Many of their books, subsequently published, are made up of discourses first preached to congregations in England, — as Cotton's at Boston, in Lincolnshire, and Hooker's at Chelmsford. The trend and prevalent topic of preaching in Puritan circles generally is well indicated in the attempts vainly made by the king and the anti-Puritan church dignitaries in England to suppress what they accounted an inordinate dealing with the abstruser and darker problems of divinity. Already, in 1622, some four years before Mr. Hooker's entrance on his Chelmsford Lectureship, James I. issued injunctions to the clergy through Archbishop Abbot, forbidding any one of them under the stand-

CALVINISTIC PREACHING. 17

ing of "a bishop or a dean to presume to preach in any popular auditory on the deep points of predestination, election, reprobation; or of the universality, efficacy, resistibility, or irresistibility of God's grace."

This was a blow at a general feature of Puritan preaching. Its insufficient result may be judged, however, by the fact that, in 1628, Charles I. felt constrained to follow up his father's plainly disregarded inhibition by another, commanding all preachers to avoid any discussion in the pulpit of any religious opinions which were not justified by, or which should seem to imply departure from, the "literal and grammatical sense" of the Articles of the Church.

When, therefore, the New England fathers and mothers are found standing on this shore of the untraversed continent, undertaking here to plant new towns and colonies, and to extend the boundaries of a Christian civilization, we must not imagine too much of a break with things of the past. If antecedent convictions on the part of a comparative few, and the force of circumstances on the part of a far greater number, did lead them to strike out a new theory in ecclesiastical affairs, and to some extent in political matters, their religious convictions and their religious life were, nevertheless, altogether homogeneous with that of a multitude of English men and women of their time at home. These, remaining behind, held by ties of family, of business, and all the hundred-fold bonds which fasten men to native land, were, not less than the voluntary exiles to this soil, true offspring of the Reformation movement; had drunk deep into its profounder spiritual springs; loved the stronger and abstruser of its doctrines; and, though destined still to pass their days in the land of their birth, in communion with, and in more or less of sympathy with, the National Church, or to endure hardness and tribulation by separation from it, were, nevertheless, at one in heart and in general type of religious life and experience with Pilgrims and Puritans on these American shores. Religion for them all meant the same thing.

What, then, looking now somewhat more narrowly at the matter, were some of the characteristics of that type of religious life brought with them by New England's progenitors to this land, and exemplified by the first generation or two in these new plantations in the wilderness?

One feature of that religious life was its profound sense of the Divine Sovereignty. The aspect in which God was conceived of was dominantly that of absolute and irresistible authority. The will of God was not only the ultimate cause of all physical and moral events, but was the foundation of morality itself. Things were not right or wrong by any inherent or necessary character in themselves; they were so because made so by the fiats of an infinite Ruler.

John Norton, successively minister of the church of Ipswich, and of the First Church of Boston, thus expresses this belief, in his "Orthodox Evangelist,"[1] — a book designed, as its titlepage tells us, as a "help for the Begetting and Establishing of the Faith which is in Jesus": —

"God doth not will things, because they are just; but things are therefore just, because God so willeth them.... What reasonable man but will yeild that the being of the Moral Law hath no necessary connexion with the Being of God? ... That the actions of men, not conformable to this Law, should be sin: that death should be the punishment of sin ... these are the constitutions of God, proceeding from him, not by way of necessity of nature, but freely, as effects and products of his Eternal good pleasure."

This sovereignty of God, so antecedent to and supreme over even moral distinctions, reached irresistibly to all events, however great, however minute. Nothing could escape its grasp and its effectual control. Not the airiest imagination, not the seemingly freest choice, but was firm-held in the vice-like clutch of a determinative purpose of the Most High. Of course there was endeavor to save the divine character in reference to the origin and continual existence of sin. Very acute are the distinctions of John Norton, chief dialectician among the New England ministers of the first generation, between the operations of God's will as a "first Cause" and the operations of man's will as a "second Cause." But what did such attempted distinctions amount to,

[1] pp. 147, 149.

when the reader of his hair-splitting explanations read also such plain allegations as these:[1] —

"He [God] so determineth the Will, as the Will determineth it self. God so determineth the Will, as a first free Agent, as that the Will determineth it self as a second free Agent. . . . The external, transient, efficacious Motion of God upon the Will, determineth the will with a real determination: the Will so moved, moveth it self with a real, and formal determination."

Plain must it be that, so far as conceptions of the divine sovereignty like these prevailed to influence the character of the religious life begotten in connection with them — and they prevailed very largely in the theory of religion, certainly — they must have shed over that life an aspect of fatalism, and have presented the truth of the divine sovereignty in one of its most perplexing and depressing possible aspects.

That they did not avail more powerfully to deject and sadden the spirits of the time we must mainly ascribe to two causes. *First*, to that happy fact, constantly to be borne in mind respecting many theories of devout men and women, that the practical issue of extreme doctrines entertained is not always, or even pervasively, what it logically ought to be. There is a reserve of sound, saving sense and feeling in human nature which often rescues life and behavior from the consequences of the most positively accepted intellectual conclusions.

[1] *Orthodox Evangelist*, pp. 114, 115.

EFFECT OF THE DOCTRINE.

And *secondly*, there was an immense offset to any inordinately depressing conceptions of divine sovereignty, as there always is when a comfortable assurance is entertained at the same time that that sovereignty is enlisted in one's own behalf or is pledged to the success of an enterprise in which one is engaged. This personal assurance in their own individual cases, it is to be believed, these good men and women very generally had. Certainly, the duty of such assurance was inculcated by their religious teachers as an almost indispensable associate or result of saving faith; if not, indeed, — as was the case with many of the Continental and English reformers, — as of the very essence of faith itself. Nor was the confidence in God's enlistment on the side of the New England enterprise one which any common measure of adversity could at all disturb. That was a thing they did not themselves question; and they suffered no one else over whom they had moral or physical control to question it either. Few offenses awoke quicker indignation or brought quicker judgment than the offense of speaking against, or sending home to England letters against, the prospects of the New England colonial enterprise. Every one of the colonies affords examples of the wrath of the people at speeches thus uttered, or reports forwarded to England, adverse to the full assurances entertained of civil and ecclesiastical success. It was in this spirit that they appropriated and cheerily sung, amid the log-huts of their scattered villages, their rude rendering of the strong old Hebrew strains: —

"He said I'll give thee Canaan's land,
   by lot heirs to be there,
When few, yea very few in count,
   and strangers in 't they were.

" He suffered none to do them wrong,
   yea, Kings for them checked he;
Touch ye not mine anointed ones,
   my prophets harm not ye.

" He also thence did bring them forth,
   with silver and with gold,
And there was not among their tribes
   a feeble person told.

" He of the heathen people did
   the land on them bestow,
The labor of the people they
   inherited also."

Still, granting all the sustaining power there always is in the persuasion that Providence is on our side, and finding in it not only a comforting fact generally but a specially explanatory and comforting fact in relation to the particular generation of people we are speaking of, there remains, nevertheless, the incontestible certainty that there must have brooded over those settlements in the wilderness a conception of the Sovereignty they were under, which, if not depressing, was at least majestic and awe-inspiring in its grandeur and sublimity.

Another conception powerfully affecting the religious life of the period under consideration was the view almost universally inculcated and, theoretically at least, as universally entertained, of man's helplessness. Man was helpless, indeed, in all moral matters; but he was especially helpless in that transcendently important but infinitely necessary business of a regenerative change of heart. The passivity of the soul in regeneration was a generally affirmed doctrine with the divines of the Reformation. Here in New England, John Norton called it [1] "a fundamentall truth" of the Gospel.

But how it was practically inculcated, we may perhaps see in the most lively way by listening to words of less didactic setters-forth of the matter, — words of men distinguished rather as preachers than as theologians. Speaking of the impossibility of a man's doing anything toward his own salvation, Thomas Shepherd says [2]: —

"Oh thou mayest wish and desire to come out sometime, but canst not put strength to thy desire, nor indure to doe it. Thou mayest hang down thy head like a Bulrush for sin, but thou canst not repent of sin; thou mayest presume, but thou canst not beleeve; thou mayest come half way, and forsake some sins, but not all sins; thou mayest come & knock at heaven gate, as the *foolish virgins* did, but not enter in and passe through the gate; thou mayest see the land of *Canaan*, & take much pain to goe into *Canan*, and mayest tast of the bunches of Grapes of that good land, but never enter into *Canaan*, into Heaven, but thou liest bound hand and foot in this woful estate, and here thou must

---

[1] *Orthodox Evangelist*, p. 281.
[2] *Sincere Convert* (1646), p. 71.

lie and rot like a dead carkasse in his grave, untill the Lord come and rowle away the stone, and bid thee come out and live."

So Thomas Hooker:[1]—

"I expresse it thus, look as it is with the wheele of a clock, or the wheele of a Iack that is turned aside, and by some contrary poyse set the wrong way. He now that will set this wheele right, must take away the contrary poyse, and then put the wheele the right way; and yet the wheele doth not goe all this while of it selfe, but first there is a stopping of the wheele, and a taking away of the poyse; and secondly the wheele must be turned the right way, and all this while the wheele is only a sufferer: so it is with the soule of a man . . . God by a holy kind of violence, rendeth the soule of a poore sinner, and withall by his almighty power, stops the force of a mans corruptions, and makes the soule teachable, and framable to the will of God: it makes it to lie levell, and to be at Gods command: and this is done by a holy kind of violence."

Or again, from the same writer[2]:—

"This union that is betwene the soule and its corruptions is marveilous strong and firme, nay so strong and firme that there is no meanes under heaven, no creature in the world that is able to breake this union, and dissolve this combination that is betweene sinne and the soule, unless the Lord by his Almighty power come and break this concord and conspiracy. . . . As it is with the body of a man, if there were a great and old

---

[1] *Preparing for Christ* (1638), pp. 24-26.
[2] *Ibid.* (1638), pp. 138-140.

distemper in a mans stomacke, if a man should put a rich doublet upon him and lay him in a Featherbed, and use all other outward meanes, this would doe him noe good. . . . Iust so it is with the soule of a man; a mans heart will have his sinne; there is an inward combination betweene the soule and sinne; now all meanes, as the Word, and the like is outward, and can doe no good in this kind; they cannot break the union betweene a mans heart and his corruptions . . . unlesse the Lord by his Almighty power and infinite wisedom make a separation betweene sinne and the soule, and dissolve this union."

This the Lord occasionally did. Hopefully He had done it, indeed, for most of those who had been gathered in this wilderness; but the proportion of men for whom He did it was relatively small, as Thomas Shepherd is strenuous in reminding his trembling, unconverted hearers [1]: —

"Now doe not thou shift it from thy selfe, and say, *God is mercifull.* True, but it is *to very few*, as shall bee proved. 'T is a thousand to one if ever thou bee one of that small number whom God hath picked out to escape this wrath to come."

But even when God did sovereignly and graciously interpose to afford the indispensable aid, the general belief of the period, and indeed the general experience of the time, made the process by which a comfortable hope of salvation was arrived at an arduous and protractedly painful one. The religious life of

[1] *Sincere Convert*, p. 98.

the time was keyed to the expectation of such agonizing experiences, and could hardly credit the genuineness of any other.

Thomas Shepherd bluntly declares [1]: —

"*Iesus Christ* is not got with a wet finger. It is not wishing and desiring to be saved, will bring men to heaven; hells mouth is full of *good wishes*. It is not shedding a teare at a Sermon or blubbering now and then in a corner, and saying over thy prayers, and crying God mercy for thy sins, will save thee. It is not *Lord have mercy upon us*, will doe thee good. It is not comming constantly to Church; these are easie matters. But it is a tough work, a wonderfull hard matter to bee saved."

The necessity of this careful, protracted antecedent process, argued at length in John Norton's treatise, already referred to, is well intimated in the heading of its sixth chapter: —

"There are certain Preparatory works coming between the carnal rest of the soul in the state of sin, and effectual vocation; Or, Christ in his ordinary Dispensation of the Gospel, calleth not sinners, as sinners, but such sinners; i. e. qualified sinners, immediately to believe."

This qualifying of sinners, as Mr. Norton phrases it, by antecedent experiences of minutely analyzed and carefully discriminated character, was generally insisted on by all preachers of the period, but perhaps found its most developed expression in the sermons and writings of that most powerful of them all in the cogency and acuteness of his pulpit deliv-

[1] *Sincere Convert*, p. 150.

erances — Thomas Hooker. Mr. Hooker has whole volumes on these experiences of the soul in process of conversion, but antecedent to conversion. They were not the product of his New England ministry only. He preached them in his Esher and Chelmsford parishes before he came here, and nothing in the way of spiritual analysis ever surpassed their anatomizing of the moral phenomena so generally regarded as indispensable to conversion. He brought to this work a subtlety of perception, a power of spiritual vivisection, an amplitude and variousness of illustration, and an energy and incisiveness of expression which were absolutely wonderful.

Mr. Hooker's emphasis upon the nature and necessity of this preparatory work may have been even then regarded as somewhat excessive. We have certainly the reported remark [1] made to him by shrewd Nathaniel Ward, of Ipswich, author of the "Simple Cobbler of Agawam": "Mr. Hooker, you make as good Christians before men are in Christ as ever they are after; would I were but as good a Christian now as you make men while they are but preparing for Christ."

Certainly, on one other point, elaborately insisted on by Mr. Hooker, and inculcated also by his son-in-law, Thomas Shepherd, he was not supported by the general convictions of his ministerial cotemporaries. His own intense experiences and his impassioned, however powerful, nature led him to promulgate a doctrine which, a hundred years later, was similarly

[1] Giles Firmin's *Real Christian* (1670), p. 19.

promulgated by a man of somewhat kindred intellectual make, and to which there will be occasion in a later lecture again to refer, — the doctrine of the necessity of such an unconditional submission of the will to God as carries with it a willingness to be lost. This doctrine, which has passed into New England theological history as a tenet of Hopkinsianism, was, a century before Hopkins, as clearly and cogently — and in far more thrilling rhetoric — stated, argued, and illustrated by Mr. Hooker.[1] It added, there can be no question — for testimony to this fact remains — as it always does, a new difficulty and terror to the processes of an inquiring spirit treading the anxious road of conviction and conversion. Mr. Hooker's view, in this particular, was disavowed

[1] Cotton Mather (following his father, Increase, in the latter's prefatory letter to Solomon Stoddard's *Guide to Christ*) attempts to defend Mr. Hooker from the imputation of teaching this doctrine, on the ground, as he sets forth in *Magnalia* i. 315, that the publication of Mr. Hooker's writings was to a great extent " without his consent or knowledge; whereby his notions came to be deformedly represented." The defense is well meant, but it is idle. The Hopkinsian doctrine of contentment in being damned was inculcated by Hooker and Shepherd with the utmost distinctness. It is not by any supposition of incorrect short-hand reporting that the doctrine can be got out of Hooker's *Soules Humiliation* or Shepherd's *Sound Beleever*. The doctrine is logically woven into the texture of both treatises. It appears and reappears in both of them. It is prepared for, led up to, stated, enforced, and objections to it answered. There is no accidental and inconsiderate slipping into its utterance. It is accepted with full intelligence and with full recognition of its obnoxiousness and its difficulty to the average experience. Pages could be quoted from both authors in support of these statements, but it is sufficient here to refer to Hooker's *Soules Humiliation* (1638), pp. 98-115, and to Shepherd's *Sound Beleever* (1645), pp. 141-155.

by John Norton in the "Orthodox Evangelist,"[1] and is not to be found in any utterance of John Cotton; while it was made — in 1670 indeed, twenty-three years after Mr. Hooker's death — a main point of opposition, in Giles Firmin's "Real Christian,"[2] to what that writer deemed the difficulty enhancing teachings of both Hooker and Shepherd in the matter of the conversion of men to Christ.

But, whatever minor notes of dissent from particular extreme views presented by any New England divine may be discovered, the general character of religious instruction in the period we are considering could not but result in a type of the religious life marked by the most minute and rigorous introspection. Both in the pulpit and in the closet, as inquiries preliminary to union with one of these wilderness churches, or as searching out ground of comfort in the solitary soul, the most merciless laying bare of personal experience was expected and demanded. Especially all the evasions and windings of the human spirit in recoil from the stern presentations made of the sovereignty and righteousness of God, were followed with microscopic acuteness and pitilessness of exposure. Holding to the immense difficulty of saving conversion, the vast liability to deception about it, together with the infinite misery of failure in the enterprise, the whole process was tried as by fire.

These spiritual experiences were publicly disclosed to the church as the basis of admission to fellowship,

[1] Page 151.   [2] Chapters i.–iv.; pp. 1–150.

and as a test by which fitness for such fellowship should be tried. A series of about fifty such "Relations," as they were called, remains, in the very difficult handwriting of Thomas Shepherd, which were presented by candidates for admission to his own church in Cambridge, — examples, from a quarter of a page to eight pages in length, of a method of scrutiny and revelation universal in the churches.

Such earnest self-inspection as characterized the religious life of this period ought, logically, one might suppose, to have resulted in a type of piety morbid as well as intense; mystic and debilitating, as well as devout and fervent. That it did not do so to any considerable extent was owing to several mutually coöperating causes.

One of these is to be found in the essential soundness and healthiness of that English temperament which our fathers and mothers inherited, and which in some good measure they transmitted to their posterity. This balanced and sober natural disposition, which characterizes our Anglo-Saxon race, is capable of subjection to intense emotions, for protracted periods of time, without losing — except in here and there individual instances — its substantially sane and just estimate of realities and its judicial self-control. Neither ecstatic and passionate with the Gaul and the Italian, nor mystic and sentimental with the German, it remains relatively rational and equipoised under the pressure of even the intensest political or religious causes of excitement, and bears, without the results which often seem their inevitable logical consequences, the impact on mind and heart of beliefs or of emergencies that appear altogether suited to drive men to enthusiasm or despair.

Another correction of any tendency to a morbid and debilitating result from the introspective training of our Puritan period of history existed constantly in the absolute necessity for the most strenuous outward activity in the labors of new-settlement life in the wilderness. This necessity existed, of course, in the conflicts with the rude and gigantic powers of nature under the altered conditions of climate and agriculture, and commerce and life generally, in this raw, new land.

But it was not nature's oppositions alone which led them outward from too great concentration upon the phenomena of the individual spiritual life. The world by which they were surrounded was not an insensate world merely, difficult to subdue because of its unplastic and intractable earthiness. It was a world under the power of malign and opposing spiritual agencies. Curiously united, in the minds of the men and women of that generation, with the high doctrines they entertained of the Divine Sovereignty were the conceptions they also held of the pervasiveness and activity of diabolic agency. The power of the devil in this new world was, after all, the chief adverse power they had to contend against. They wrestled not so much against flesh and blood, against frost and storm, and drought and flood, as against him whose malignant spirit these things were largely taken to represent, and whose stronghold, tyrannized over by him for centuries, they had had the hardihood to invade. The solemn primeval forests were tenanted with spectres, demons, and emissaries of the evil one. Their trails and footprints infested every pathway through darksome glen or over rocky hillsides; and every unusual accident, or perilous misadventure, or misdirection in the tangled thickets, or loss or illness of cattle, could be traced to their malicious mischief. The poor Indians of the native woods were Satan's special slaves and victims, and efforts made to convert them excited his peculiar ire. It was to revenge these assaults upon his vassals and his domain that the crops of the settlers were cut off by frost, that fevers invaded their homes, that their fishing barks sank in the turmoiled waters of rivers and the sea.

The shadow of this enmity of spiritual foes lay like a cloud over the whole landscape of the spiritual life. We get a little glimpse of the intensity of its occasional gloom, and of the terrors which might sometimes be roused by it, in the scenes which took place in connection with the witchcraft persecutions, for the most part at a period considerably later than the epoch now spoken of. "For the most part," it is remarked, since much earlier than the time of what we call the Salem delusion, even as early as 1648, in Hartford, six months after Hooker died, a woman had been hung for familiarity with the devil.

But all this apprehension of Satanic interposition in common affairs, if it served no other good purpose, gave an outward tendency to men's thoughts which

SATANIC OPPOSITION. 33

largely offset the influence of the introspective habitudes which were inculcated as so necessary to safety in spiritual things. And it is certainly a signal tribute, alike to the courage and the self-forgetfulness of the piety of our progenitors, that, in spite of what they deemed the peculiar dangers of the enterprise, and the special oppositions of Satan engendered by it, such earnest and successful endeavors to Christianize the Indians — that is, to rescue them from the direct and exclusive control of Satan — were made by the early churches of New England.

But more influential doubtless than any other cause in steadying, and, on the whole, reasonably guiding the course of religious conduct in the Puritan period, — indeed, deserving to be set by itself as one distinct feature of the religious life of the time, — was the place accorded in men's belief and behavior to the authority and to the universal applicability of Scripture.

The Reformation recoil from the centralization of authority in the priesthood and the Church had resulted in the enthronement of the printed Scriptures in the seat of absolute supremacy. Far more than any previous epoch of Christian history had ever witnessed, the volume called the "Word of God" was now made the final arbiter of doctrine and of conduct. And it was not only finally authoritative, but it was universally applicable also. Equally, in all portions. it was the explicit utterance of the infinite Wisdom and Will; and a text taken from it anywhere, which seemed to fit appropriately any given question or situation, was viewed as doubtless the decisive utterance of the mind of God concerning it. The New Haven congregation certainly, and other congregations probably, rose and remained uncovered while the pastor solemnly pronounced the text of his discourse, having in those syllables listened to the immediate accents of the Holy Ghost. That colony explicitly adopted the Scriptures as "a perfect rule" of government in civil as well as in religious affairs; and in all the colonies an appeal to Scripture was held valid in support or in contravention of every proposed item of legislative enactment or judicial procedure.

Held thus as the regulative guide in all civil concerns, the Scripture was of course supreme and unquestionable in spiritual matters. To its last syllable of history or of pedigree it was vitally pregnant with deepest religious meaning. All there was of Godhead crowded itself into each utterance of prophecy, narrative, or proverb. Isaiah or Ecclesiastes, Genesis or Solomon's Song, were weighted down with living present meaning, suited to men in all the passing exigencies of those troubled days.

Indeed, it may be said by way of digression, there is something exceedingly interesting and almost pathetic in the special feeling toward this last-named book — the Jewish Love Song — which the Rabbis of the Hebrew Synagogue prohibited the reading of by their neophytes till they were past forty years of age.

These good men and women in this hard wilderness, like their harassed and troubled religious brethren and sisters in English trials at home, found in the luxurious imagery, the passionate language, and the joyous and loving utterances of this book attributed to Solomon, what was undoubtedly a most welcome contrast to the hard narrowness of their ordinary surroundings and their common thought. With perfect purity and simplicity of feeling they seized upon it, spiritualized it, adopted it, and lived in it, as a delightsome pleasure ground of the soul, of which Christ was the central figure, and of which the Church's love to Christ and his love to the Church was the perpetual theme. So that, in the midst of this howling wilderness and all the strenuous hardships of their days, few books of Scripture were more resorted to for texts, for sermons, or for comfort in private devotion than this. It is with something of admiration as well as wonder that we picture them in their rude sanctuaries, sitting sex by sex apart on the hard benches, in torrid summer heats or fireless winter colds, listening devoutly and fervently as their minister read : —

"As the lily among thorns, so is my love among the daughters. As the apple-tree among the trees of the wood so is my beloved among the sons. . . . He brought me to the banqueting house and his banner over me was love. . . . His left hand is under my head, and his right hand doth embrace me. I charge you, O ye daughters of Jerusalem, by the roes and by the hinds of the field, that ye stir not up, nor awake my love, till he please."

THE PURITAN PERIOD.

The generally accorded authority and finality ascribed to the Scriptures, however sometimes that Scripture was fancifully or extravagantly interpreted, was, on the whole, a very steadying and controlling power in repressing individual enthusiasm and eccentricity in religious matters. An outward standard, accessible to all and familiar to all, was close at hand by which faith and conduct were to be tried. And, as long as that standard remained unchallenged in its exclusive and solitary sufficiency, no mere questions of interpretation, less or more violent or fantastic, could very seriously disturb the homogeneity of faith.

It was for this reason, undoubtedly, as being only a matter of Scripture interpretation variant from that of the churches generally, that William Pynchon's book on the Atonement no more violently moved the people of the time on its publication in 1650. Mr. Pynchon, the founder of Springfield, and a merchant of high repute, wrote a book on the "Meritorious Price of Christ's Redemption," which in some of its features anticipated, by about one hundred and thirty years, what, since the days of Jonathan Edwards the younger, has been known as the New England theory of the Atonement.

It was a book which ought to have marked an epoch in New England theology. It did make considerable stir among the preachers of the time and the leaders among the legislators. But it treated Scripture as reverently as any other volume did, and hence did not profoundly disturb the general mind of the people, or apparently enlist very much of their concern. The book appealed to Scripture; and the legislature of Massachusetts set John Norton to reply to it out of Scripture. He did so in a very elaborate volume. The legislature also ordered the heretical book to be burned; and so the incident closed, its only conspicuous results being that it retarded for a hundred and more years that view of the Atonement which has been generally accepted for the last three generations among New England churches, and that it made Mr. Pynchon's book so scarce that a copy of it readily sells for four or five hundred dollars.

But once touch the authority of Scripture, and there was another sort of matter on hand.

Very interesting is it to note, therefore, that it was precisely at this point of the treatment of Scripture that the two disturbing movements, which really agitated this period of religious life in New England, emerged, with something of rebellion against prevailing established conditions.

These two disturbing movements — that of Mrs. Hutchinson's promulgation of Higher Life and Perfectionist doctrines, and that of the Quakers' declaration of the Immediate Guidance of the Holy Spirit — differed, indeed, considerably from each other and were quite separate in the personalities which they represented, and in the political and social results to which they tended. But they were, after all, traceable to one root, — a different view of the authority of Scripture from that commonly entertained.

Mrs. Hutchinson's position was, however, in this respect the less definitely pronounced. Her contention with the views of the ministers and churches of the time seemed, indeed, at first, to be rather a matter of a somewhat different explanation of Scripture than anything affecting the authority of Scripture. In this aspect of the matter she drew Rev. John Cotton a considerable way in his sympathies with her. But as she went on in her public Bible-readings about faith, justification, sanctification, and especially the witness of the Spirit, the dullest ear began to suspect that it was not in expounding the Scripture only that she differed from Wilson and Davenport and Bulkley, and other " black-coats from the Ninniversity," but in things deeper than those of mere interpretation, as well. It is impossible to read the eighty-two opinions alleged to be entertained by her, and which were certainly condemned as being hers by the solemn Synod of 1637, without seeing that the fathers of the churches of that day correctly discerned in them a view of Scripture which, right or wrong, certainly differed from their own.

When the good-hearted, enthusiastic woman said, as the articles of condemnation allege she did say, — " The whole letter of the Scripture holds for a covenant of workes ; " " The due search and knowledge of the holy Scripture is not a safe and sure way of searching and finding Christ; " "There is a testimony of the Spirit, and voyce unto the Soule, meerely immediate, without any respect unto, or concurrence with the Word," — it is plain that her

SOURCES OF CONTROVERSY. 39

breach with the doctrine generally taught in the churches went farther than any question of Scripture explication only; it reached to the question of the immediacy of Divine revelations as well.

The Quakers frankly took up, on this point, the position inferentially deducible from Mrs. Hutchinson's more guarded expressions. They affirmed that Scripture was not ultimate and exclusive. The Spirit of God still lived in His Church, still communicated Himself to and inspired men. They declaimed against the ministers and the churches for putting out one eye of truth, and for shutting men up to a printed book only for spiritual guidance, when God stood ready to give Himself to every open soul.

But these revolts against prevailing views, though productive of more or less turmoil, did not seriously affect the religious life of the mass of men and women. The doctrine of the all-sufficiency of Scripture, and its finality as authority, remained substantially undisturbed.

It is often declared that a period of religious life marked by such characteristics as have been indicated must have been one of universal hardness and gloom. It has been fashionable to speak of Puritan times as joyless and hopeless, and of the lot of men, women, and children then as only and altogether miserable. The assertion is utterly inaccurate.

Whether ascribable to the happy facility of human nature, already referred to, in evading the extremer results of logical arguments, or because of the resiliency and vigor of the Anglo-Saxon constitution, or

THE PURITAN PERIOD.

because of the consolations and comforts of the grace of God in human hearts, or more probably because of all of these things with others combined, life in those Puritan days was not essentially gloomy or hard or miserable. The new-comers to this forest continent had, indeed, hard things to encounter. The times nowhere, in the Old World or the New, were those of softness or ease. Severity in the treatment of wrong-doing was the universal rule of law; mercifulness and pity toward transgression of Divine or human statutes were nowhere found. The softer side of life had not anywhere come to be much taken into account.

But that the Puritans of New England were typically hard, austere, and unhappy people, is utterly to mistake their character, and to falsify their relative standing-place among men.

Their legislation from the very outset, when compared with English legislation at home, was one of mercifulness. Twelve different offenses were, in Massachusetts and Connecticut, in 1642, regarded as punishable with death. New Haven numbered fourteen at the same date. But as late as 1819, in Great Britain, two hundred and twenty-three offenses were liable to the extreme penalty.

The numbers executed for witchcraft in New England are but a beggarly handful compared with those who so died in Old England; and while the last of these tragedies in New England occurred in 1692, they continued in Old England till 1712. Is it thought that no place was left for the tenderer emotions of conjugal and family affection? Read Margaret

Winthrop's letters to her husband for as sweet an expression of such sentiments as literature anywhere can show. Were the men of that day — untutored in literary art, as is readily granted — absorbed wholly in rigorous severities of religious thought and discipline? Read William Wood's "New Englands Prospects," and John Josselyn's "New Englands Rarities Discovered," or even Edward Johnson's "Wonder-Working Providence of Sions Saviour," and see as keen an appreciation of nature's beauties, and of the characteristic life of field and wood and sky, as, in an easier and more cultured time, was ever possessed by a Bryant or a Longfellow.

Notice how almost every one of that day who wrote at all, even the grave Governor Bradford of Plymouth, or the sage Mr. Cotton of Boston, dipped occasionally into rhyme. Why, even elegiac and epitaphal verse bristled with quip and epigram; as witness this of Edward Bulkley on the death of the pragmatic Mr. Stone of Hartford: —

> " A *Stone* more than the *Ebenezer* fam'd;
> *Stone* Splendent Diamond, right *Orient* nam'd;
> A *Cordial Stone* that often cheared hearts
> With pleasant Wit, with Gospels rich imparts:
> *Whet-Stone*, that Edgefi'd the obtusest Mind;
> *Load-Stone*, that drew the Iron Heart unkind;
> A *Ponderous Stone*, that would the bottom sound
> Of Scripture-depths, and bring out Arcans found:
> A *Stone* for Kingly Davids use so fit
> As would not fail *Goliaths* Front to hit:
> A *Stone*, an *Antidote*, that break the course
> Of Gangrene Error by convincing force;
> A *Stone Acute*, fit to divide and square;
> A *Squared Stone*, became Christs Building rare."

The men who did that sort of thing — and they were many — were not poets doubtless, but they were not religious ascetics or misanthropes either. They knew a joke as well as any one. They appreciated a pleasant turn of thought and the utterance of a kindly feeling as well as men do to-day.

It is not true that Puritan life was a life of gloom. Husbands and wives loved as they do now. Children were a joy in households as they are still. Young men and maidens had their attractions, their jealousies, their trepidations, their happy understandings at the last, as at present. About them the seasons walked in glorious change as they do yet. And they were not insensible to these things. Life was, in all its great essential verities and joys, what we find it ourselves.

And so, to bring this lecture to an end, the period closed, exhibiting still a type of piety essentially unaltered from that brought at its beginning to these shores. Its rigorous doctrines remained unabated in severity of statement; its sharp experiences in conversion were still exemplified; but then, as all along, much that seemed inevitably depressing and gloomy was offset and alleviated by activity, health, good-hearted companionship in what they deemed a great cause; by trust in God, and by community of hope and endeavor, rising to peace, and even to joy, in self-denial and suffering, for the Church's sake.

II.

THE PURITAN DECLINE.

The previous lecture attempted to set forth the characteristics and conditions of the religious life of New England's first generation, or generation and a half, of dwellers. The period considered was, in a general way, from the planting of the Plymouth Colony in 1620 to about the termination of the active lives of the founders of the later colonies of Massachusetts Bay, Rhode Island, Connecticut, and New Haven; that is to say, to about 1655 or 1660.

It was seen that the type of religious life which characteristically marked that opening period of New England history was eminent for the strenuous severity of its doctrinal conceptions; for its profound and humiliating views of human sinfulness and danger; for its searching introspectiveness into the criteria of personal religious experience; for its absolute repudiation of all dependence on outward forms as a ground of saving hope; for its reverence for the least and obscurest phrase of Scripture; and, in general, for its intensity and seriousness, passing over sometimes into austerity and superstition.

The period whose type of religious life is now to be considered stands, to a considerable extent, in contrast with that just described. And yet, in saying this, and characterizing it, for want of any better name, as the period of Puritan Decline, too much or too sharp contrast must not be supposed to lie between them. Large masses of people do not change their religious attitude instantly or universally. The alteration is gradual; and it is for the most part by insensible and individual changes that things come to be what they were not before. And, moreover, there are always those so conservatively constituted that they hardly appear to change at all. So that, characterize any given period of history accurately as one may, there are some of its constituent personalities and elements which cannot possibly be brought within its general terms of designation, and which may always be held up as objections to the correctness of that designation.

Still, on the whole, and in a large significance of the phrase, the period of which we are now to think, and which reaches from about 1655 or 1660 to 1735, — three score and fifteen to four score years, — cannot be otherwise denominated than as one of religious declension.

Perhaps no better approach to the examination of the period now in question can be had than through the doorway of a paragraph or two from a statement made, in 1701, by two old men whose lives and observations reached well back toward the commencement of New England's religious story. One of these men was John Higginson, who was born in England in 1616; came to this country with his father, Francis, the first Salem minister in 1629; taught school in Hartford in 1638; then preached at Guilford for several years, but settled in 1660 at Salem over what had once been his father's church, where he sustained a pastorate of nearly half a century, till his death, in 1708, terminated a ministry of seventy-two years. He was, at the period of his Testimony, eighty-five years of age.

The other man was William Hubbard, also born in England, in 1621; who arrived in this country in 1635; graduated in the first class sent forth from Harvard College in 1642; and occupied an honorable pastorate at Ipswich for forty-eight years. Here he wrote a History of New England, indorsed by the Massachusetts General Court; and, at the date of his uniting with Higginson in a public declaration of their joint convictions on the religious situation, was eighty-one years of age. I will quote only a few sentences from this remarkable and pathetic document.

"Above *Seventy* Years[1] have passed away, since one of us, and above *Sixty* since the other of us came into *New-England;* and *having obtained Help from God, we continue to this Day.*

"We are therefore Capable to make some *Comparison*, between the Condition of the Churches, when they were first *Erected* in this Country, and the Condition into which they are now *Fallen*, and more *Falling* every day.

"But we wish, that in making this *Comparison*, we had not cause to take the place, and the part of those *Old Men*, that saw the *Young Men, Shouting aloud for Joy*, at the

---

[1] *A Testimony to the Order of the Gospel, in the Churches of New England* (1701).

New-Temple. Ezra 3 : 12. *Ancient men that had seen the First House; when the Foundation of this House was laid before their Eyes, Wept with a loud Voice.* We are under a daily Expectation of our call to appear before our Lord Jesus Christ; and we have reason to be above all things concerned, that we may *Give up our Account with Joy* unto Him. That we may be the better able to do so, we judge it necessary for us, to leave in the Hands of the Churches, a brief Testimony, to *the Cause of God, and His People* in this Land. And this the rather, because we are sensible that there is Risen and Rising among us, a Number who not only forsake the *Right wayes of the Lord,* wherein these Holy Churches have walked, but also labour to carry away, as many others with them as they can. . . . . And this we Declare with the more concern upon our minds, because of an Observation, so plain, that *he that runs may Read it.* It is too observable, That the *Power of Godliness,* is exceedingly Decaying and Expiring in the Country."

We might, perhaps, take these utterances of Higginson and Hubbard as the sad retrospective expressions of advanced age looking backward on past times as better times, were it not for the fact which meets us in so many forms, — in sermons, in legislative enactments, in proclamations of executive officers, in records of criminal prosecutions, as well as in solemn ecclesiastical assemblies called to put a barrier to growing evils in church and society, — that the statement of the old men in their Testimony was not only true, but was generally recognized as being true.

Already, twenty-two years before this time of the old men's Testimony, a Synod, — called by the General Court of Massachusetts, and known from the attempt it made to redress the evils which occasioned its summons as the "Reforming Synod," — had, in 1679, put on record its acknowledgment of a "great and visible decay of the power of Godliness" in the churches. It pointed out in minute and elaborate specification among the evils of the time, and which were believed by the Synod to have brought Divine judgments upon the country, those of neglect of Divine worship, disregard of sacramental observances, pride, profanity, Sabbath-breaking, family lawlessness and irreligion, intemperance, licentiousness, covetousness, and untruthfulness, as largely prevailing and characterizing the period.

There is manifold and incontestable evidence from every quarter that the indictment, pathetically brought against the generation to which the two old men addressed their dying appeal, had in it a tremendous weight of truth; and that the state of things in view of which it was spoken, and which was prolonged for years after their ineffectual voices had become silent, was in many ways contrasted, in its prevalent type of religious life, with that which had characterized the first generation or two of New England dwellers.

But, though the main object of the present lectures is to analyze and depict the characterizing features of the religious life prevailing at different epochs of New England history, rather than to set forth at large the causes which, from time to time, wrought alterations in those features; still, in the case of the present period, as in that which went before and in those which will follow, some glance at the influences which combined to change the type of religious life from that which previously prevailed, may be the shortest road to an appreciative understanding of the type itself.

One influence, then, which wrought powerfully to alter the tone of religious feeling brought by the first-comers to this land to one of a lower level, grew out of the inevitable facts of life in a new, undeveloped country. The first settlers, coming from the comparatively cultivated ways of their European homes, and coming, too, under the impulse of high motives and aspirations, could in their own persons largely resist the deteriorating tendencies of sordid surroundings, meager social privileges, scant educative opportunities; and some, through the power of their high moral intent, could even turn the very lack of these things oftentimes to spiritual advantage. But it was very different with their grandchildren. These had to grow up in destitution, to a great extent, of adequate schooling, or of proper instruction in the common amenities of life. The fathers did, indeed, considering the age and the exigencies of their situation, manifest a heroic courage and foresight in their attempts to establish schools, and even to found a college almost at the very first. It was only 1636 when the General Court of Massachusetts ordered the beginning of Harvard College. It was only 1642 when the same authority took common schools at public cost into legislative care. Connecticut Colony had provision for such schools before 1642, and New Haven Colony in 1641.

Lord Macaulay, in 1847, made a famous address in Parliament, eulogizing as one of the most remarkable of historic events this early recognition by "exiles living in a wilderness," of the great "principle that the State should take upon itself the charge of the education of the people." Well might he do so, for this principle never was fully recognized in England till the year 1870.

But it was easier for the fathers liberally to plan than fully to execute. Life pressed hard on them. The demands of daily toil were exacting and depressing. The school privileges afforded in the scattered townships were necessarily scanty in amount and meager in quality. The common intercourse of men took on a tone of rudeness, characteristic always of pioneer life and separation from the softening and civilizing influences of long established communities.

The descendants, too, of a class of people quite or nearly contemporaneous with the original settlers,— their servants or adventuring hangers-on or followers, — who never had any special sympathy with the high ideals of the real fathers of the New England enterprise, had multiplied as well as the offspring of the founders themselves, and had naturally suffered more even than they from the influences which led to moral decline. They were relatively a numerous, and positively a debasing, factor in the life of the colonial towns and villages.

THE PURITAN DECLINE.

Then, too, as time went on, there was a progressive decline in that important source of educative advantage found in the utterances and influence of the pulpit. The great leaders of the New England immigration were university men. Some of them were men of national distinction in their own land. Some had had the benefit of continental travel and observation. Many of them came of families of long recognized standing and worth. Cotton Mather enumerates[1] seventy-seven ministers of the early New England churches who began their ministry in the old country, and who must have been, nearly without exception, graduates of the highest educational institutions of their English home. And some of their hearers, like Winthrop and Bradstreet and Vane, were scholars of the same universities.

But these men one after another died. The provision they had wisely made for the perpetuation of a godly and learned ministry availed, indeed, to prevent the New England pulpit from ever becoming a feeble one, or one not distinctly educative and superior in its leadership of the time. But there was, speaking generally, a decline.

And there was more decline in the pews. The number of well-educated laymen showed a still greater relative disparity as the years went by. Evidences of this popular falling off of intelligence are very familiar to every one who has had occasion to examine the handwriting and the spelling of wills, deeds, and public records of the period now

[1] *Magnalia* (ed. 1820), pp. 213–215.

EDUCATIONAL DECLINE. 51

in question, compared with that which went before. This nearly universal token of the degeneracy just spoken of is well illustrated in the indorsement made on Governor Bradford's manuscript History of Plymouth Colony by his grandson, Samuel Bradford, which reads as follows : —

"This book was rit by goefner William Bradford, and gifen to his son mager William Bradford, and by him to his son mager John Bradford, rit by me Samuel Bradford, Mach. 20. 1705."

The writer was a lieutenant, a selectman of Duxbury, a juryman, and an important citizen ; but he spelled the title of his grandfather the honored governor, " goefner," and that of his father and brother the majors, " mager "; given became " gifen "; and there were various other personal aberrations of orthography.

So that, quite apart from the operation of any other causes than those necessarily inherent in the gravitating tendency of frontier experiences and the inevitable deprivations and hardships of a raw, new country, it is not surprising that life, in all its dignities and adornments, stood at a distinctly lower level than it had done from fifty to seventy years before.

Meantime, to an extent perhaps not generally remembered, the people of the period under consideration were almost wild with what may be called the land-grabbing spirit. No modern Oklahoma or Cherokee-strip invaders can surpass the fervor of those New Englanders of the period from 1660 to 1735, in their desire to get possession of the good spots of unoccupied territory. It was the great town-planting epoch of our New England history. A hundred and nine of the present townships of Massachusetts, and more than eighty of Connecticut, date their settlement or their arrival at the dignity of incorporation in the seventy-five years now under review. Companies for the purchase and settlement of new townships were formed in every considerable community. To get more and more land was the consuming endeavor of the hour. Of course this impulse but extended and aggravated the evils of frontier life already spoken of,—evils which might, in some measure, have been corrected had the people been content to settle down more compactly to the improvement of the communities already established. But the anticipatory Western fever was on them; and to get further into the woods seemed a passion.

There were other causes, also, which powerfully and unfavorably affected the conditions necessary, or at least especially desirable, for healthy and progressive religious life. The period was one of almost continuous political anxiety, and often of active military strife.

The epoch opened with the solicitudes attendant upon the restoration to power in England, in 1660, of that Stuart dynasty to escape whose earlier tyranny the founders of these colonies had come to these shores; and with consequent apprehension of peril to their chartered liberties. The colonists had courage and fidelity to welcome and secrete the regicide judges, Goffe, Whalley, and Dixwell; but they did it with trembling, lest it bring down upon them the penalty of a revocation of every accorded civil privilege.

With the years 1675 and 1676 came that most desperate of all our New England Indian struggles, known as King Philip's War, which carried ravage and fire around the whole circumference of the colonies, though having its chief seat in eastern Massachusetts and in Rhode Island.

Upwards of six hundred of the flower and strength of the youth and middle age of the land perished in that short but tremendous struggle. Twelve or thirteen towns were entirely destroyed, and about six hundred buildings burned; while the colonies, enfeebled in productive manhood, found themselves burdened by oppressive debt.

The year 1684 saw issued out of the English Chancery the long-dreaded writ of forfeiture of the Massachusetts charter; and 1685 beheld proceedings looking toward a similar action against Connecticut. The year following brought Sir Edmund Andros to Boston with a commission for the immediate government of all New England; an attempted exercise of which authority in Connecticut was attended in Hartford, in 1687, by the excitements and tumults accompanying the hiding of the charter in the ever since historic Charter Oak.

The accession of William and Mary, in 1689, brought relief, indeed, from the machination of Andros; but it brought also the responsibilities of participating with the Mother Country in a French war, and the expedition against Quebec in 1690.

The years 1692 and 1693 cast over eastern Massachusetts in particular, and over all New England in some degree, the awful shadow of the witchcraft prosecutions, in which more than a hundred women, not to speak of many men, mostly of the fairest character, and many of them of excellent families, were arrested, examined, and generally imprisoned, as in complicity with the Devil. Nineteen executions by hanging of persons thus adjudged guilty, and one person pressed to death for refusing to say whether he was guilty or not,— doubtless because he saw the uselessness of a denial, and hoped thus to save his property for his family, — evidenced, in Massachusetts alone, the terrible power of a delusion which it was felt might break out at any time and anywhere, and against which the purest character and the most intimate family ties were powerless to defend. Thirty years before, the Connecticut Colony had been the scene of a somewhat similar excitement, though on a lesser scale, in which at least six persons were hanged, and several others condemned.

Queen Anne's War broke out in 1703, and with it the horrors of Indian incursion, one incident of which was the assault on Deerfield, in 1704, the massacre of forty-seven of its inhabitants, and the transport to Canada of a hundred prisoners, including Rev. Mr. Williams, who saw his invalid wife tomahawked not many furlongs from his burning house. The colonists retaliated these incursions by an expedition along the Penobscot and Passamaquoddy shores even as far as Port Royal. This French stronghold was again approached, and vigorously, though unsuccessfully, assaulted in 1707, but was at last captured in 1710. The next year, 1711, saw the expedition by land and sea against Canada, and its abortive conclusion.

Meantime, all along during these exciting scenes of political agitation, social disturbance, and military struggle, the feeble colonists had been harassed and oppressed by laws of the home government, laying heavy burdens on their commerce, and treating them as sources of enrichment to English enterprise and to the national treasury, rather than as infant commonwealths, to be protected and developed in healthful growth. These disadvantages were still further aggravated, especially for the Massachusetts Colony, by the disastrous experiments of that province in paper currency. Up to the date which has been set as the close of the period under survey in this lecture, namely, 1735, Connecticut had not suffered much from this cause of trouble. Her turn came, however, a little later. From these early New England experiments in finance, some of our present-day political leaders, one might suppose, could learn a very instructive lesson. Not a scheme now advocated as a brand-new method of securing what our politicians delight in calling an "elastic but stable currency, with every dollar equal to every other dollar," but had then its supporters. A currency based on interchangeable commodities ; a currency based on real estate; a currency based on the credit of commercial associations,—all had their advocates. But then, — as always, till a fresh lesson of calamity teaches its peril anew,—fiat money was the popular form of finance, and the form resorted to. Fiat money was issued in great quantities during this period in Massachusetts, and a little later in Connecticut, with the result of momentary inflation and quickly following collapse of all commercial enterprise, shrinkage of all actual incomes, hardship, and disaster.

Then too, Nature, or Providence, seemed to conspire with human foes to awaken distress and alarm. Violent hurricanes repeatedly ravaged the slight-built towns and destroyed shipping along the coasts. The years 1663, 1727, and 1737, were marked by alarming earthquakes. In 1676, Boston was visited by a fire which burned up forty-five dwelling-houses, the North Church, and several warehouses,—an experience which, in 1679, was repeated on a larger scale in the destruction of eighty dwellings, seventy warehouses, and several vessels at the wharves, entailing a loss of two hundred thousand pounds. Epidemics of small-pox raged in 1692, 1700, and 1721, and diphtheria, known as "throat distemper," swept across the country in 1700, and again in 1735.

Meantime, coming closer to things distinctively religious, men's minds were agitated out of that general agreement as to what was true and right in religious belief and practice which had, to so great an extent, characterized a previous generation, and which seems so largely essential to the development of any pervasive type of religious character. The occasions of these agitations were various.

One of them, early in the period at present under survey, grew out of the presence and prophesyings in various parts of New England of the Quakers, and the witness borne by them against what they claimed to be the errors of an ecclesiastical tyranny.

These protests were often almost insane in their extravagance of language, as well as in their offensiveness and sometimes indecency of manner; but the undeniable sincerity out of which they sprang, and the heroic patience with which their promulgators endured cruel stripes and imprisonments, and even death, in support of their convictions, made an impression, nevertheless, and awoke questionings in many minds which did not give utterance to speech, concerning the infallibility of that spiritual guidance under which New England found itself.

It was not without its deeply disquieting influence, after various other lesser severities had been visited upon a large number of earlier offenders of this sect, that, at the close of the Thursday lecture on the 27th of October, 1659, the people of Boston saw three condemned persons, — William Robinson, Marmaduke Stevenson, and Mary Dyer, — marched between a file of soldiers on either hand to the place of execution. The prisoners had been warned out of the Bay Colony under the terms of a statute which sentenced Quakers to banishment, and, if banishment was disregarded, to death.

Mary Dyer walked between the two male prisoners, hand in hand with them, with shining face and uplifted eyes, radiant as to a wedding hour. The drummers were placed close to the prisoners to drown their voices if they should attempt to address the people. Thirty-six sentinels were stationed about the town to preserve order, and to give notice of any attempt at outbreak against the authorities; for many of the townsmen, who had no sympathy with Quaker doctrines, and who were disgusted with Quaker extravagances and pretensions to prophetic light and authority, were even more shocked at the cruelty of the treatment to which they were subjected. Arrived at the gallows, Mary Dyer was reprieved — reprieved only for a time; for, being sent out of the province, she returned in May following, again to be sentenced, and at that time actually to die. Her two companions were hanged, and their bodies put in a shallow hole in the ground without coffins, or other vestments than those they wore to execution. Sympathizing Quaker friends came to the spot a day or two after, and were permitted to disinter the bodies and robe them somewhat more decently for the grave, but were not allowed to furnish coffins.

Such scenes as this strained, fully as tautly as it would bear, the bond of allegiance of many to their political and religious guides, and awoke more problems by far than they settled in the people's minds.

Later, somewhat similar questionings arose, occasioned by the spread of Baptist principles. It had not been without its occasion for stir in people's thought that, as early as 1654, Henry Dunster, the first President of Harvard College, had been compelled to retire from that institution for adopting the Baptist idea of church-membership. And now, in spite of legislative enactments and of ecclesiastical denunciation, Baptist churches were increasing in all the colonies. It is true that their members, except of course in Rhode Island, were under social disadvantages, and were taxed for the support of religious institutions in which they did not believe, and imprisoned when they would not pay the tax; but still they and the controversy grew.

A Baptist church edifice was erected in Boston almost surreptitiously — that is, the proposed object of the edifice was kept a secret while in building — in the year 1679. Its erection was the signal of violent outcry against the promoters of Baptist sentiments on the part of the regular, that is, the Congregational, ministry, and was the occasion of a distinct reference in the Result of the Synod of 1679, before spoken of, as being "an altar" set up against the "Lord's altar." So great was the opposition aroused that, in March, 1680, the promoters of the enterprise were brought before the Court of Assistants; and, because they would not promise to cease from their undertaking, the magistrates ordered their church doors to be nailed up. This, of course, — human nature being what it is, — did not tend to allay excitement about Baptist principles or very much retard their growth.

Moreover, and still more alarming in the view of

many, because backed by governmental and ecclesiastical authority from abroad, attempts were being made to introduce into New England a form of church-government which it had been the distinct object of some of the colonists in coming here to escape; and which others, through their observations and experiences on this soil, had rejoiced to have left behind. An Episcopal congregation, with all its characteristic claims to be the only true church in the place, was formed in Boston in 1686. An English society for the purpose of the " Propagation of the Gospel [that is to say, Episcopacy] in Foreign Parts" was organized in 1701, with direct intent to carry the system established by law at home into the American dependencies of the Crown. The first fruit of this enterprise in New England was the founding of an Episcopal mission at Stratford, Connecticut, in 1706; while a still more startling token of the Society's activity was found in the announcement made to the Trustees of Yale College at the Commencement in September, 1722, that the rector of the College, its tutor then in office, and five neighboring Congregational ministers, were on the point of receiving Episcopal orders.

But, unfavorable as some of these things were in themselves, and all of them in the disquietude accompanying them, to the prevalence and growth of a high and uniform type of religious life among the people generally, still it may be doubted whether any one of them was so influential in letting down the tone of religious principle and behavior as a cause

THE HALF-WAY COVENANT. 61

which yet remains to be spoken of, and which, like many other errors of good but short-sighted men, grew out of an honest attempt to serve the interests of piety and of the Church.

This cause of religious declension was the operation of the Half-way Covenant.

The fundamental principle of the founders of the New England churches in coming out from the National Church of the old country, was that a church should be composed only of recognizably regenerate souls. As Thomas Hooker phrased the doctrine:[1] "Visible Saints are the matter," and "confederation the form," by which only a true church can be constituted.

But with this principle, which certainly implied discernible Christian character and intelligence enough to enter into mutual covenant, was associated the additional doctrine that the children of visible confederated saints were themselves also church-members and saints; and of course that their children also would be so in their turn. This did well enough so long as the children of the first covenanting parents were children, and the question of their saintliness remained a hypothetical matter. But how when they grew up to manhood and womanhood, and were consciously and visibly no saints at all, in that interior and self-scrutinizing sense which was generally admitted as necessary to eternal life? Where did such people stand? Would the best way to treat them be to abandon any theory

[1] Hooker's *Survey*, Preface.

which asserted the membership of children with their parents in the church at all, and to deliver them over to the "uncovenanted mercy" of their Maker,— and to the machinations of the Devil;— or would it be better to adhere, at least in part, to the theory which had been conscientiously held of their church connection, so endeavoring to retain them and their offspring in visible association with the people of God, while nevertheless limiting their privileges as church-members, as not being fully qualified for participation in all rites? The question was long and earnestly and most conscientiously debated. In ministerial correspondence, in ecclesiastical assembly, and finally in a governmentally called Synod, the problem of the relation of the children of church-members to the Church was discussed.

The conclusion finally reached, and gradually accepted throughout the Congregational churches of New England, was that such children were to this extent church-members, and visibly in covenant by reason of their baptism in infancy, that they in turn could present their children for the reception of the same rite; but that neither they nor their children could be accounted full members, entitled to participate in the Lord's Supper, or in the voting privileges of the church. For these things a further experience and an additional act of public consecration were requisite. Two forms of covenants thus came into use in enrolling the membership of the churches,— one for the full-membership of those who professed and gave evidence of spiritual change; the other for those who did not profess to go so far as that, but only covenanted practically to do the best they could, and to bring up their children to do likewise. Hence the nick-name "Half-way" Covenant, expressive of the limited profession and partial membership of those who entered into it.

But, however conscientiously devised, this scheme wrought inevitable mischief to the spiritual life of the period we are considering. It afforded a sort of easy resting-place for people between utter neglect of religion and full surrender to its claims. It gave to parental instincts the solace of a kind of commendation of their children to God, which did not, however, imply the entire surrender by the parents of their own hearts, nor an expectation of their children's surrender. It cheapened disastrously the conception of the privilege and responsibility of church-membership itself; and, more disastrous still, it turned attention to that which was in nature most contrary to the Puritan idea, — the observation of a form, and trust in a ceremony, on the part sometimes of a chief portion of those who were nominally connected with the church. So that the curious spectacle came to be witnessed of a people, who two or three generations before had come out from a foreign land and from home and church-relationship as a protest against formalism, becoming, by the period of which we are speaking, in reference to a very large part of their posterity, distinctly formalistic.

This formalizing tendency in religion, characteristic of this period, received a large impulse, moreover, from a cause less distinctly marked in its origin than the ecclesiastical arrangement we have just considered; namely, a gradual and insensible, but progressive, change in the directions uttered from the pulpit as to the method of entrance on a religious life. There was as yet little dissent in New England from the old-time inculcation of the helpless passivity of the soul of man in the crisis of conversion. But with the decline of the spiritual intensity of the earlier generation, and with decreasing examples of that religious transformation once so frequent and so volcanic in quality, enhanced attention was turned to those things which might be accounted likely to promote, or at least to put a man in advantageous position for, the accomplishment in him of a work he was powerless himself to perform. No man could make himself a Christian; but there were things he could do, which would perhaps render it more likely that he would divinely and irresistibly be made one. He could pray. He could go diligently to church. He could catechise his children. He could even, if he had been baptized himself in infancy, in the judgment of the very eminent Solomon Stoddard of Northampton, and of a considerable number of other distinguished pastors, partake of the Lord's Supper, though consciously unregenerate, as one of the means by which, or in connection with which, the converting grace might possibly descend upon his soul.

It will be easily seen how readily, in a time of

FORMALIZING TENDENCIES. 65

general religious decline, the emphasis of religious exhortation would change from entreaties to be at once repentant and believing, to admonitions to make use of means for becoming so. Nor is it less obvious how direct would be the tendency of exhortations of this character to fix primary attention on the means, rather than the end, and to formalize religion by elevating a routine of external behaviors into so prominent a place in spiritual affairs.

Such progressive externalizing processes did widely mark the character of pulpit inculcations. Largely resulting from an honest but mistaken theory of church-membership, — itself accommodated to the exigencies of an unforeseen situation, — and promoted by a declension which the ministers strove against, but found themselves powerless to resist, the type of religious life of the period now in question took on an aspect of formality and indifference which certainly would have filled the first colonists with amazement.

Taking all these things together, — the degenerative tendencies of frontier and new-settlement life; of Indian warfare and political anxiety; of depressing financial disasters and alarming prevailing disease; of religious controversies and the contentions of sects fought out, not in the arena of moral debate only, but in the legislature, the court-room, and the jail; and, adding to these things a vicious theory of the Church itself on the part of that body which represented the great and authoritative portion of the community as a whole, — is there any reason to wonder that the period under present consideration should have been one of religious decline? Such a decline we might say, apart from other causes alone, was almost deserved as a proper retribution for the uncharitable severity with which conscientious dissent from the established views was treated even by the best of our New England fathers. True, the principle of toleration in religious matters was almost nowhere recognized in those days. England had none of it. Holland alone had it in considerable extent. And it is the very point of severest indictment against our New England intolerance that many of the planters of these colonies had enjoyed the benefit of Holland's liberality in these matters, and ought to have learned a little of the lesson of a forbearance they had needed so much in their English home, and which the experience of some of them on Dutch soil might have taught them how to exercise. If religion itself declined, we cannot acquit them of all responsibility for its decadence.

Plenty of evidence remains of the earnest struggle of the great body of the ministry of that day against a condition of things that it was almost powerless to resist. It was not Higginson and Hubbard only who discerned and deplored the low estate of religion; the same lament appears in almost every utterance which has come down to us from that time. In 1668 Rev. William Stoughton preached the Election Sermon before the governor and legislature of Massachusetts. In it he said:—

THE DECLINE RECOGNIZED.

"O what a sad *Metamorphosis* hath there of later years passed upon us in these Churches and Planta- tions? . . . Alas! how is *New England* in danger this day to be lost even in *New-England* ? To be buried in its own Ruines? . . . The first generation have been ripened time after time, and most of them geathred in as *shocks of corn in their season*. . . . Whilest they lived their Piety and Zeal, their Light and Life, their Coun- sels and Authority, their Examples and Awe kept us right, and drew us on in the good wayes of God, to pro- fess and practise the best things; but now that they are dead and gone, Ah how doth the unsoundness, the rot- tenness and hypocrisie of too many amongst us make it self known, as it was with *Joash* after the death of *Jehojadah*. . . . It is a sad name to be styled *Children that are Corrupters;* but are we not indeed many of us *corrupted*, and which is far worse *Corrupters?*"

Preaching the next year, on a similar occasion, before the General Court of Plymouth Colony Rev. Thomas Walley said : —

"Are we not this Day making Graves for all our Blessings and Comforts? Have we not Reason to ex- pect that e're long our Mourners will go up and down and say, *How is New England fallen ? The Land that was a Land of* Holiness, *hath lost her* Holiness? *That was a Land of* Righteousness, *hath lost her* Righteous- ness? *That was a Land of* Peace, *hath lost her* Peace? *That was a Land of* Liberty, *is now* in sore Bondage?"

In May, 1670, Rev. Samuel Danforth was the preacher of the Election Sermon in Massachusetts.

He called on the magistrates, clergy and people assembled on the occasion to consider : —

"Whether we have not in a great measure forgotten our Errand into the Wilderness. You have solemnly professed before God, Angels and Men, that the Cause of your leaving your Country, Kindred and Fathers houses, and transporting your selves with your Wives, Little Ones and Substance over the vast Ocean into this waste and howling Wilderness, was *your Liberty to walk in the Faith of the Gospel with all good Conscience, according to the Order of the Gospel, and your enjoyment of the pure Worship of God according to his Institution, without humane Mixtures and Impositions.* Now let us sadly consider whether our ancient and primitive affections to the Lord Jesus, his glorious Gospel, his pure and Spiritual Worship and the Order of his House remain. . . . Let us call to remembrance the former dayes, and consider whether *it was not then better with us, then it is now.*

" In our first and best times the Kingdome of Heaven brake in upon us with a holy violence, and every man pressed into it. What mighty efficacy and power had the clear and faithful dispensation of the Gospel upon your hearts? how affectionately and zealously did you entertain the Kingdome of God? How careful were you, even all sorts, young and old, high and low, to take hold of the opportunities of your Spiritual good and edification?, ordering your secular affairs . . . so as not to interfere with your general Calling. . . . Then had the Churches *rest*, throughout the several Colonies, and were *edified: and walking in the fear of the Lord, and in the comfort of the holy Ghost, were multiplied.* O how your *Faith* grew exceedingly! you proceeded from faith to faith, from a less to a greater degree and measure, growing up in Him who is our Head, and receiving abundance of grace and of the gift of righteousness. . . . O how your *Love* and *Charity* towards each other abounded! O what comfort of Love! . . . what a holy Sympathy in Crosses and Comforts, weeping with those that wept, and rejoycing with those that rejoyced!

"But who is there left among you, that saw these Churches *in their first glory*, and how do you see them *now?* Are they not in your eyes in comparison thereof, *as nothing?* . . . Is not the Temper, Complexion and Countenance of the Churches strangely altered? Doth not a careless, remis, flat, dry, cold, dead frame of spirit grow upon us secretly, strongly, prodigiously? They that have Ordinances, are as though they had none; and they that hear the Word, as though they heard it not; and they that pray, as though they prayed not; and they that receive Sacraments as though they received them not; and they that are exercised in the holy things, using them by the by, as matters of custome and ceremony . . . Pride, Contention, Worldliness, Covetousness, Luxury, Drunkenness and Uncleanness break in like a flood upon us, and good men grow cold in their love to God and to one another."

In 1678, Dr. Increase Mather, pastor in Boston, and soon after President of Harvard College, also, published a treatise entitled, "Pray for the Rising Generation," in which he said : —

"*Prayer* is needful on this Account, in that *Conversions* are becoming *rare* in this Age of the World. They that have their Thoughts exercised in discerning Things of this Nature have had sad apprehensions with reference to this Matter; That the *Work of Conversion* hath been at a great Stand in the World. In the last Age, in the Days of our Fathers, in other Parts of the World, *scarce a Sermon preached* but some *evidently converted*, and sometimes *Hundreds* in a *Sermon*. Which of us can say we have seen the like? *Clear, sound Conversions* are not frequent in some Congregations. The *Body* of the *rising Generation* is a *poor, perishing, unconverted*, and (except the Lord pour down his Spirit) an *undone Generation*. *Many* that are Profane, Drunkards, Swearers, Lacivious, Scoffers at the Power of Godliness, Despisers of those that are Good, Disobedient. *Others* that are only civil, and outwardly conformed to good Order by Reason of their Education, but never knew what the *New Birth* means."

So little, however, had matters improved, twenty-two years later, that Increase Mather wrote again in his " Order of the Gospel," published in 1700 : —

" If the begun *Apostacy* should proceed as fast the next thirty years as it has done these last, surely it will come to that in *New England* (Except the Gospel itself *Depart* with the *Order* of it) that the most Conscientious People therein, will think themselves concerned to gather Churches out of Churches."

Rev. Samuel Torrey of Weymouth, Massachusetts, preaching the Election Sermon in May, 1683, called on his hearers to consider : —

" That there hath been *a vital decay, a decay upon the very* Vitals of Religion, by a deep declension in the Life,

and Power of it; that there is already a great *Death*
upon Religion; little more left than *a name to live;* that
the *Things which remain, are ready to dye;* and that we
are in great danger of dying together with it."

After summoning attention to the " dying of Religion " in " Churches " and in the " Hearts of its
Professors," he goes on : —

" How is Religion dying in *Families!* through the
neglect of the religious Service and Worship of God,
and of the religious Education of Children and Youth
in Families. Truly, here, and hereby, Religion first received its death's wound. Hence Religion is dying in
all other Societies, among all Orders and Degrees of
men, in all ways of Converse, both Civil and Ecclesiastical. O there is little, or nothing of the Life of Religion to be seen, or appearing either in the Frame, or
Way; Hearts or Lives of the generality of the Professors of it."

So, too, it looked to Rev. Samuel Willard, preaching, in 1700, on the " Peril of the Times Displayed,"
and looking from the standpoint of his Vice-Presi-
dency of Harvard College, as well as from the pulpit
of the South Church in Boston. He says : —

" How few thorough Conversions are to be observed?
How scarce and seldom? Men go from Ordinance to
Ordinance, and from year to year, and it may be they
are sometimes a little touched, awakened, affected, . . .
but how few are there who are effectually and thoroughly
turned from sin to God. . . . Bad *Symptoms* . . . are
upon the rising *Generation.* It hath been a frequent

observation, that if one Generation begins to decline, the next that followeth usually grows worse, and so on, till God poureth out his Spirit again upon them; . . . The decayes which we do already languish under, are sad, and what tokens are there on our Children that it is like to be better hereafter? . . . God be thanked, that there are so many among them that promise well. . . . But alas, how doth vanity and a fondness after new things abound among them? how do young persons grow weary of the strict profession of their fathers, and become strong disputants for those things which their progenitors forsook a pleasant Land for the avoidance of!"

Nor were signs of such declension of the religious life at all limited to the Massachusetts and Plymouth colonies. In Connecticut, judged by all tokens, the decline was just as obvious.

Rev. Samuel Mather of Windsor, writing in 1706, says in a pastoral letter addressed to his people:[1] —

"It is a time of much Degeneracy. . . . In great measure we in this Wilderness have *lost our first love.* . . . We do not walk with God as our Fathers did, and hence we are continually from year to year under his *Rebukes* one way or other; and yet alas, we *turn not unto him that smites us:* these considerations call for the utmost of our endeavours, for the reformation of what is amiss amongst us: and for the upholding and *strengthening of what yet Remains,* and is perhaps *ready to dy.*"

[1] Dedicatory Epistle prefaced to *The Self-Justiciary Convicted and Condemned,* pp. 3, 4.

THE DECLINE RECOGNIZED.

Across the river, at East Windsor parish in the same town, Rev. Timothy Edwards — father of the great Jonathan — preached a sermon in May, 1712,[1] on a topic upon which the condition of things about them impelled the ministers of Farmington, Hartford, and Windsor unitedly to agree, namely: "Irreverence in the worship of God, and prophanation of his Glorious and fearfull Name by Causless Imprecations and Rash Swearing."

Two years later, in 1714, Rev. Samuel Whitman of Farmington preached the Election Sermon in Hartford before the General Court. In it he said:

"Is not Religion Declining? Indeed 't is too Evident to be denied, that Religion is on the Wane among us, 'T is Languishing in all Parts of the Land.... Time was when the Ordinances of God were highly-Prized; Our Fathers had a high Esteem of them, and laid great Weight on them.... But now, the Love of many to them is grown Cold. They have as low an Esteem of them, as the Jews had of their Manna, their Bread from Heaven, when it fell every Night about their Tents.... Is not Religion degenerated into an empty Form?... Does not Pride abound among us? Not meerly Pride in Apparel; many going above their Estates and Degrees: but a Haughtiness of Spirit that shows itself in many ways; In a Contempt of those that are by far their Betters: The Child behaving himself Proudly against the Ancient, the Base against the Honourable.... We are risen up a Generation that have in a great Measure forgot the Errand of our Fathers."

[1] Stoughton's *Windsor Farmes*, p. 139

The subject and the spirit of the Election Sermon, preached by Stephen Hosmer of East Haddam before the Connecticut General Court, in 1720, is well indicated in its title : "A People's Living in Appearance and Dying in Reality."

Following in the same strain on a like legislative occasion, in 1730, Rev. William Russell of Middletown, from the text in Revelation: "I have somewhat against thee, because thou hast left thy first love," challenged his hearers as to an unquestionable fact: —

"Don't the generality of Professors among us savour of Vanity, Worldliness, Pride, and discover great Unthoughtfulness of God? How little of that Seriousness, Humility and Heavenly-mindedness, that was in some of our Predecessors? . . . The Country improveth in Knowledge and Skill in Worldly business, but in Religious Knowledge, doth it not manifestly decay? . . . And is there not abundance of Unrighteousness & Unmercifulness among us? Injustice in Prices, delays and dishonesty in Payments, Deceit, Falseness, and Unfaithfulness in Bargains, Contracts and Betrustments, griping Usury, Evading and Baffling the Laws made for the Security of men from that Oppression? a multitude of Law Suits, Men ready to take one another by the Throat?"

We should be glad to consider such melancholy utterances as the somewhat professional expressions of men who, because of their clerical positions, were more liable than others to take a somber view of the moral condition of the community about them.

Unfortunately we cannot do this. The evidence in all quarters — civil proclamations, court procedures, jail accounts — is against so lenient a conclusion. Well-nigh all old church records bear witness to an almost incredible laxity of morals in the regions with which they have to do. They are melancholy reading, except for the fact that they plainly indicate that strenuous attempts were made to stem the evils which they reveal as existing. The sins chiefly disclosed by them are those of intemperance, lying, slander, and licentiousness; the latter especially prevalent among the younger parts of the community, on that border-ground of half-way relationship to the Church which has already been described. It is a painful matter to refer to; but so marked a blemish on the moral and religious life of the time cannot be overlooked.

A very frequent antecedent to admission to the covenant, or of advancement to full communion, was public confession of repentance for sins of unchastity previously committed. Almost all old church records preserve more or less instances of the kind; some of them very many.

One occasion, doubtless, of the necessity of taking cognizance of misbehaviors in this most rudimentary point of morals, was that curious custom — long happily obsolete in New England at least, but once, owing probably to meager sitting-room accommodations and inadequately warmed houses, largely prevalent in these commonwealths — the custom of young people prosecuting what was intended to be, and doubtless generally was, a proper acquaintance and courtship, tucked up together in a bed. Of course the young companions were presumably clothed in their ordinary attire; and nothing was further from the intention of the establishers or the promoters of this curious social usage than the endangerment of morals. Attempts have been made to ascribe this custom to only the very lowest order of people. But this is idle. Jonathan Edwards, preaching in his own pulpit in that always rather aristocratic New England township of Northampton, bluntly says:[1]—

"I desire that certain customs that are common among young people in the country, and have been so a long time, may be examined by those rules that have been mentioned. That custom in particular, of young people of different sexes lying in bed together! However light is made of it, and however ready persons may be to laugh at its being condemned . . . whoever wisely considers the matter must say, that this custom of this country . . . has been one main thing that has led to that growth of uncleanness that has been in the land."

The evidence is only too abundant that the custom was one of extensive prevalence, and that it was the unhappy, however unintended, occasion of the tarnishing of multitudes of New England church records, and the blotting of many a fair name

[1] *Works* (ed. 1809), vol. vii. p. 150.

among not the least honored of our New England families.¹

Certainly, with the increase of drunkenness, profanity, and licentiousness, which all available sources of information plainly indicate as marking this period, a great change had taken place from a condition of things which enabled the author of "New Englands First Fruits" to say, in 1643: "One may live there from year to year, and not see a drunkard, hear an oath, or see a beggar;" or which justified Hugh Peter, on his return to England from his American home, in saying, in a sermon preached before Parliament, the Westminster Assembly of Divines, and the Corporation of the City of London, in 1646: "I have lived seven years in a country where I never saw a beggar, nor heard an oath, nor looked upon a drunkard."

But there was one token of a certain change in the religious feeling of the people, extending progressively through this period, which, partly because it was of a more interior and elusive character, and partly because it was in one instance at least connected with a conspicuous ecclesiastical movement, may appropriately claim a moment's more definite notice.

---

¹ This unpleasant, but historically practical, subject has been treated of with suitable discretion in a little volume entitled, *Bundling; its Origin, Progress and Decline in America*, Albany, 1871, by H. R. Stiles, M.D. All readers of old church records will, however, acknowledge that Dr. Stiles has not over-stated the gravity of the practice in question and its prevalence at the period reviewed.

It was remarked in the previous lecture that the practice of giving "relations" of experience, as a preparatory step in entering into church-membership, was universal in early New England history. These relations, as was then said, were often of the most minute and introspective kind. The practice, initiated in a period of great religious emotion and naturally expressive of it, was continued after that emotion had largely cooled; indeed, in modified and various forms, it continues generally among most of our churches to this day.

But there gradually developed, as the conditions of feeling changed, an alteration in the minds of many as to the expediency and necessity of such presentations, before the eyes or ears of others, of the processes of men's minds and hearts in personal religious experience. And, in 1699, at the establishment of a new church in Boston — the Brattle Street Church — among other innovating procedures which threw the ecclesiastical circles of that region into very considerable turmoil, was an innovation on this time-honored and generally accepted usage.

The eighth article of the Declaration of the new church was as follows: —

"But we assume not to our selves to impose upon any a Publick Relation of their Experiences; however if any one think himself bound in Conscience to make such a Relation, let him do it. For we conceive it sufficient, if the Pastor publickly declare himself satisfied in the person offered to our Communion, and seasonably Propound him." [1]

This innovation awoke considerable opposition on the part of the general body of the Massachusetts clergy, and would very likely have been fruitful of more lasting consequences had not the pastors of the Brattle Street Church been, as events proved, successively evangelical and devout-hearted men; so that, notwithstanding relations may have been formally dispensed with, there is good reason to suppose that pastoral solicitude and inquiry practically secured in that church (at least while Colman and the elder Cooper lived) all that was secured by the older method in the other churches of the time.[2]

The spirit of dissatisfaction with the requirement of such relations was, however, abroad. Relations were still customarily presented by applicants for church-membership; but their tone was greatly modified. A less strenuous type of individual feeling, as compared with that expected in the early days of these churches, was regarded as sufficient evidence of qualification for church-fellowship. The state of public sentiment about the matter was

[1] See Lothrop's *Brattle Street Church*, pp. 20-26, for the somewhat warlike "*Manifesto or Declaration, Set forth by the Undertakers of the New Church now Erected in Boston, in New England, November 17th 1699.*"

[2] See Mr. Brooks Adams's *Emancipation of Massachusetts*, pp. 237-254, for an altogether amusingly exaggerated account of the significance of the whole Brattle Street transaction.

probably fairly indicated in the letter written to his people in Windsor, Connecticut, by the faithful though invalid Samuel Mather, in 1706, which has already been quoted from in another connection. He says:[1] —

"I might particularly add a few Words about a matter concerning which there is a growing agitation in diverse Places; & perhaps some in *This Place* are not so well satisfyed, *viz.* Concerning Persons making of a Relation; or giving some account of the Work of Grace upon their hearts, in order unto their being admitted into full communion in the Churches where they dwell. It is well known what hath been, and what is the practice of the Church in this place."

And then, in advocacy of the old and once spontaneous way, he goes on : —

"I might tell you how that One Relation hath begot another: and how One told me some years ago, that among the scores that he had heard read in Publick, he had never heard one, but what made him to tremble, because, in them all he found matter of Conviction in coming short of any such Work, as some others had experience of."

All which necessity of argumentation only shows the reality of the change that had come over the general tone of religious feeling since the former times.

On the whole, in spite of the fact that there were, unquestionably, as truly devout men and women as

[1] Preface to *Self-Justiciary*, pp. 16, 17.

EFFECTS OF THE DECLINE.

in religion's earlier days in New England, and that the endeavors of many godly ministers to stem the downward tendency of affairs were really heroic, there can be no question that the period which we have been reviewing was one of religious declension throughout New England. It was marked by a lessened intensity of spiritual experience in the really devout, and by a far greater indifference to the sanctions of truth and the demands of duty in that large body of people who, while nominally connected with the church by covenant, made no pretension to a regenerate life. Outward questions of ecclesiastical administration, of politics, of war, of land acquisition and new settlement, distracted people's minds from the concentrated attention once given so earnestly to religious concerns. The corrupting influence of association with Indians — who were always easily seduced with drink, and whose women were often open to solicitations of their chastity — undermined the morals of a great number of young and middle-aged men in all the provinces; while war and border conflicts roughened and demoralized many others, exposed to camp life and its inevitable temptations.

Formality in the churches had been developed, to a degree at which the fathers would have wondered, by the prominence which had been attached to baptism as the means of keeping a people in visible covenant with God, even when destitute of the actual power of godliness. And, while there had been no largely recognizable change in the doctrinal instructions of the pulpit, — as, indeed, there had been little interest in doctrine, as such, since the fathers brought a generally accepted type of it to these shores, — there had been an insensible falling off in the strenuousness of the presentations of doctrinal teachings; an increasing insistence on the value of religious observances; and an enhancing emphasis — for which there certainly was need — on inculcating what the leading spirits of the era which we are next to consider were accustomed to stigmatize as the " mere Arminian moralities " of life.

The sudden awakening from this apparent torpor of the religious sense, in a period shortly to follow, will be the topic of the next lecture.

III.

THE "GREAT AWAKENING" AND ITS SEQUELS.

FROM the condition of formalism and declension which, to so great an extent, marked the religious life of New England for upwards of two generations previous to 1740, the churches were aroused, about that date, by a spiritual quickening of so distinct and pervasive a character that it has passed into history as the "Great Awakening." Some anticipatory signs of such possible revival of spiritual energies had been manifested here and there at intervals for some years previous.

Even as early as the winter of 1704–05, under the earnest ministry of Rev. Samuel Danforth of Taunton, Massachusetts, a remarkable religious quickening occurred in that place.

Writing under date of February 20th, Mr. Danforth says:[1]

"We are much encouraged by an *unusual* and *amazing Impression*, made by GOD'S SPIRIT on *all Sorts* among us, *especially* on the young *Men* and *Women*. It's almost incredible how many visit me with Discoveries of the *extreme Distress of Mind* they are in

[1] *Christian History*, June 4, 1743.

about their *Spiritual Condition.* . . . We are both, *Church,* and all *Inhabitants* to *renew* the *Covenant* for *Reformation,* this *Week;* which this people made with God, the last *Philip Indian War.*"

In the following March, Mr. Danforth writes again, telling how " three hundred Names " were, at the meeting appointed, " given in *to list under Christ,* against the Sins of the Times ; " and that " a hundred more," detained from that meeting, could also covenant in like manner. But it rather surprises us that, with this general stir in the community and this readiness to make engagement against the " Sins of the Times," Mr. Danforth is able only to report fourteen persons as presenting themselves for church covenant, and but part of these for full communion.

Similar stirrings of religious emotion occurred several times in the ministry of Rev. Solomon Stoddard of Northampton; conspicuously in 1712 and 1718, when we are told[1] " the *bigger* Part of the *young* People in the Town, seemed to be mainly concerned for their eternal Salvation." In the year 1721, the town of Windham, Connecticut, under the pastoral care of Rev. Samuel Whiting, was visited by a marked awakening.

More general, though, it is to be apprehended, more ephemeral in its results, was the stirring of religious feeling through a considerable part of New England, occasioned by the earthquake of October 29, 1727.

[1] *Christian History,* June 4, 1743.

Writing of the effect of this startling event in the region under their observation, Rev. Messrs. Sewall, Prince, Webb, and Cooper of Boston, say :[1] —

"When God arose and shook the Earth, his *loud Call* to us in that amazing Providence, was follow'd, so far as Man can judge, with the *still Voice* of his SPIRIT, in which he was present to *awaken* many . . . and to *turn not a few* from Sin to God in a *thorough Conversion.*"

Nevertheless, the reverend writers feel compelled to record that "much the greater Part of those whom God's Terrors affrighted" made "speedy Return to former Sins."

Much more prophetic of the general awakening which was to come was the revival at Northampton and many adjacent towns in Massachusetts, as well as in several towns in Connecticut, in the years 1734, 1735, and 1736.

The occurrences in Northampton were probably the most striking in themselves of the phenomena of this movement, as certainly they are the best known by reason of the eminent powers of observation and narrative possessed by Jonathan Edwards, their delineator. Of the results in that place Mr. Edwards says : [2] —

"If I may be allowed to declare any thing that appears to me probable in a Thing of this Nature, I hope that *more than three Hundred* Souls, were *savingly* brought home to *Christ*, in this Town, in the space of *half a Year.*"

[1] *Christian History*, June 11, 1743.   [2] *Ibid.*, June 18, 1743.

He speaks of admitting "about an *hundred*" to communion before one Sacrament occasion, and "*four-score*" at another; but he records in connection with this statement, what the careful reader of his narrative will do well to remember, that "it is not the Custom here, as it is in many other Churches in this Country, to make a credible Relation of their inward Experiences the Ground of Admission to the Lord's Supper." And not only had relations of experience been abandoned under the ministry of Mr. Stoddard,— Mr. Edwards's grandfather and predecessor,— but Northampton was the center from which the Stoddardean doctrine of the Lord's Supper, as a hopefully converting ordinance for unregenerate persons, had been promulgated; which doctrine was not repudiated till thirteen years later by Mr. Edwards. So that the admission of so many as were received to the sacrament in the Northampton revival of 1735 probably signified less than it might have done under other circumstances and in some other places.

Still, this visitation of revival influences, which at this period reached the whole line of river towns from Northfield, Massachusetts, to Windsor, Connecticut, and which in the latter colony touched places as wide apart as Stratford, New Haven, Groton, Lebanon and Coventry, was a fact of such interest that it attracted the attention of devout men in the home country; and a narrative of it, written by Mr. Edwards at the request of Rev. Drs. John Guyse and Isaac Watts, was extensively circulated in England and Scotland, as well as in America.

The attention of English Christians being turned thus to American religious affairs, and prayer for American religious welfare becoming as it had never been before a feature of English desire, the way may be said to have been in a manner prepared, both at home and abroad, for that wider religious movement which we know as the "Great Awakening" in which an eminent English evangelist was to perform so conspicuous a part.

The announced purpose of these lectures being to subordinate historic narration to the business of delineating the spiritual conditions of the religious life at the various periods under review, the attempt will not be made carefully to follow the career of Mr. Whitefield, or minutely to detail the incidents which attended his course from his arrival at Newport, Rhode Island, in September, 1740, onward through his successive visits to New England until his death at Newburyport in 1770.

The story is, indeed, a picturesque one, but it is reasonably familiar. It is enough for the purposes at present in view to note how, on his first pilgrimage through these provinces in 1740, he was attended by almost universal demonstrations of popular acclaim; was welcomed by the great majority of the ministers with cordiality to their pulpits; and how by the fervor of his impassioned oratory he stirred the general masses of the communities in which, or near to which, he delivered his enthusiastic and melting discourses, as no single voice has ever stirred New England people since that day. Beginning his almost royal progress at Newport, preaching at Bristol by invitation of the General Court, he was conducted to Boston by the son of Governor Belcher of Massachusetts, specially sent to meet him for the purpose. Here the eloquent evangelist was received into the churches with almost every conceivable token of admiration, not to say of adulation. His preaching was to houses so crowded that he had in some instances to be carried through a window over people's heads to the pulpit; his audiences numbering, according to his estimate, twenty thousand hearers at one time on the Common. From Boston he extended his pilgrimage, accompanied by similar demonstrations of approval, eastward through Salem, Ipswich, Marblehead, Portsmouth, and York; next westward through Sudbury, Worcester, Brookfield, Hadley, and Northampton; thence southward through Springfield, Windsor, Hartford, Wethersfield, Middletown, and Wallingford to New Haven; and so on through Milford, Stratford, Fairfield, Stamford, and Rye to New York. Certainly, no such ecclesiastical progress, marked by victorious oratory and popular enthusiasm, is anywhere to be paralleled in New England's religious story.

Perhaps as vivid an impression of the general feeling of expectancy and wonder among the common sort of people almost everywhere respecting Mr. Whitefield and his mission as can easily be gained may be derived from an extract from a hitherto unpublished narrative written by Nathan Cole of Kensington parish, Connecticut, who therein records his own endeavors to put himself in connection with the great evangelist.

Mr. Cole was a farmer; he became a Separatist from the ecclesiastical establishment of Connecticut Congregationalism, lived to old age, and left a manuscript account of his "Spiritual Travels" which indicates at once his illiteracy as to the schools, and his simple sincerity as to things of conscience and the religious life. He says : —

"Now it pleased god to send mr. whitfeld into this land & my hearing of his preaching at philadelphia like one of the old aposels, & many thousands floocking after him to hear ye gospel and great numbers were converted to Christ, i felt the spirit of god drawing me by conviction i longed to see & hear him & wished he would come this way and i soon heard he was come to new york & ye jases [Jerseys] & great multitudes flocking after him under great concern for their Soule & many converted wich brought on my concern more & more hoping soon to see him but next i herd he was on long iland & next at boston & next at northampton & then one morning all on a Suding about 8 or 9 o Clock there came a messenger & said mr. whitfeld preached at hartford & weathersfield yesterday & is to preach at middeltown this morning[1] at 10 o clock i was in my field at work i dropt my tool that i had in my hand & run home & run throu my house & bad my wife get ready quick to goo and

---

[1] The date was October 23, 1740.

hear mr. whitfeld preach at middeltown & run to my pasture for my hors with all my might fearing i should be too late to hear him i brought my hors home & soon mounted & took my wife up & went forward as fast as i thought ye hors could bear, & when my hors began to be out of breath i would get down & put my wife on ye Saddel & bid her ride as fast as she could & not Stop or Slak for me except i bad her & so i would run untill i was almost out of breth & then mount my hors again & so i did severel times to favour my hors we improved every moment to get along as if we was fleeing for our lives all this while fearing we should be too late to hear ye Sarmon for we had twelve miles to ride dubble in littel more then an hour & we went round by the upper housen parish & when we came within about half a mile of ye road that comes down from hartford weathersfield & stepney to middeltown on high land i saw before me a Cloud or fog rising i first thought off from ye great river but as i came nearer ye road i heard a noise something like a low rumbling thunder & i presently found it was ye rumbling of horses feet coming down ye road & this Cloud was a Cloud of dust made by ye running of horses feet it arose some rods into ye air over the tops of ye hills & trees & when i came within about twenty rods of ye road i could see men & horses Sliping along in ye Cloud like shadows & when i came nearer it was like a stedy streem of horses & their riders scarcely a horse more then his length behind another all of a lather and fome with swet ther breath rooling out of their noistrels in ye cloud of dust every jump every hors semed to go with all his might to carry his rider to hear ye news from heaven for ye saving of their Souls it made me trembel to see y^e

WHITEFIELD'S PREACHING. 91

Sight how ye world was in a strugle i found a vacance between two horses to Slip in my hors & my wife said law our cloaths will be all spoiled see how they look for they was so covered with dust that thay looked allmost all of a coler coats & hats & shirts & horses We went down in ye Streem i herd no man speak a word all ye way three mile but evry one presing forward in great hast & when we gat down to ye old meating house thare was a great multitude it was said to be 3 or 4000 of people asembled together we gat of from our horses & shook off ye dust and ye ministers was then coming to the meating house i turned and looked toward ye great river & saw the fery boats running swift forward & backward bringing over loads of people ye ores roed nimble & quick every thing men horses & boats all seamed to be struglin for life ye land & ye banks over ye river lookt black with people & horses all along ye 12 miles i see no man at work in his field but all seamed to be gone — when i see mr. whitfeld come up upon ye Scaflil he looked almost angellical a young slim slender youth before some thousands of people & with a bold undainted countenance & my hearing how god was with him every where as he came along it solumnized my mind & put me in a trembling fear before he began to preach for he looked as if he was Cloathed with authority from ye great god, & a sweet sollome Solemnity sat upon his brow & my hearing him preach gave me a heart wound by gods blessing my old foundation was broken up & i saw that my rightcousness would not save me then i was convinced of ye doctrine of Election & went right to quareling with god about it because all that i could do would not save me & he had decreed from Eternity who should be saved & who not i began to think i was not Elected & that god made some for heaven & me for hell & i thought god was not Just in so doing i thought i did not stand on even Ground with others if as i thought i was made to be damned my heart then rose against god exceedigly for his making me for hell now this distress lasted almost two years."

Something similar to this excitement attending Mr. Whitefield's preaching at Middletown attended his preaching everywhere. And there was to a very considerable extent a substantial justification for the enthusiasm felt. A quickened state of religious feeling, which here and there had broken out, as we have seen, into distinct religious awakenings, had prepared the way for the most impassioned of his utterances. His fame as an evangelist had preceded him and had enkindled anticipation of the beneficial results to follow his coming. His methods were novel, and his endowments for his undertaking certainly large. The ministers of New England at this period, with very few exceptions, preached from closely written manuscripts, which must generally have been held in the hand, and often near to the eyes, and their preaching was with few graces of manner or elocution. Here suddenly appeared among them a young man of twenty-six years of age, whom nature had endowed with some of the greatest gifts of an orator, — a splendid physique, a marvelous voice, a vivid dramatic power, — one who seemed to pour forth his torrent of apparently unpremeditated eloquence without fatigue or study. It was a novel experience to listen to such a man. American congregations had never heard the like.

And, for the most part, his utterances were such as were suited profitably to arouse and safely to guide religious feeling in his hearers. He spoke to men's spiritual wants. He depicted at once their sin and the way of deliverance from sin. His strong Calvinistic presentations of the sovereignty of God's elective purposes were softened by his fervent, if somewhat illogical, appeals to human activity in turning to repentance and faith.

There was, indeed, all along, and increasingly as his progress through the prostrate crowds of admiring listeners drew toward its close on this first pilgrimage, another side to his utterances, and one which was destined to have a serious bearing on his future influence, as well as a disastrous effect on the course of that religious awakening he did so much to arouse.

While Mr. Whitefield was eloquent, devout, and doubtless "sincere," he was also young, opinionated, and censorious. He was easily affected by the physical phenomena which sometimes attended his impassioned exhortations, — the outcries, the ecstasies, the swoonings away, — and instead of repressing them as unessential, he so treated them, recorded them, and gloried in them, that they came in the common view to be regarded as almost necessary signs of a true revival, and were, by several of Mr. Whitefield's ardent followers and imitators, extravagantly encouraged and cultivated. He gave great place and importance to sudden impulses, and, as he regarded them, direct suggestions on the mind from divine sources as to actions to be performed, or as to estimates to be made of men's character. Jonathan Edwards, riding horseback by his side from Northampton to Windsor, ventured to suggest to him that he gave too great heed to such things. The suggestion was very coolly received; and though there was no break between them on account of it, Mr. Edwards records:[1] "I thought Mr. Whitefield liked me not so well for my opposing those things." Mr. Whitefield lent also the great weight of his influence to a harsh and censorious judgment of his fellow-ministers, especially any who did not at once coöperate with him in his characteristic measures, declaring them blind and unconverted. So sweeping and denunciatory were his judgments — to the extent even of deliberately writing down in his journal[2] at the close of his first New England tour, that, in his opinion, "many, nay most that preach, do not experimentally know Christ" — that an inevitable reaction took place in the minds of some who had at first yielded their judgments to his control. Then, too, good, painstaking men were willing to be guided, and even to be reproved, by this gifted youth; but, conscious of their own integrity and the sincerity of their motives, they did not relish, nor could they be expected to relish, a general denial, before their congregations, of their Christian character and their proper place in the Christian ministry.

[1] *Letters to Clap.* [2] *Seventh Journal*, p. 56.

Mr. Whitefield's unfavorable estimates of New England's religious guidances went beyond the pulpits, and enveloped in condemnation the two colleges. Of these he said:[1] "Their Light has become Darkness, Darkness that may be felt."

These harsh and divisive utterances of Mr. Whitefield were aggravated in their effect by the conduct of very many subsequent participators in the evangelistic itineracy which shortly became a marked feature of this epoch. Several of these itinerating evangelists were men whose piety and sincerity none could question, though there were those even among these whose discretion was certainly open to doubt; while in the cases of Rev. Gilbert Tennent and Rev. James Davenport something more than indiscretion characterized utterances whose direct influence was to alienate congregations from their pastors, and to stimulate and encourage whatever was extravagant in the emotions of their hearers. But this itineracy on the part of the ministry — itself a new thing in New England, and, rightly or wrongly, looked upon with disfavor by the more conservatively inclined — was supplemented by a lay itineracy, entirely novel in New England, and certainly not always either devout or wise. We are vividly reminded of a condition of things in England a century previous, in the last years of Charles I. and the days of the Commonwealth, when a like confusion of functions in worship extensively prevailed. A hostile and criticising, but substantially truthful, memorial of the

[1] *Seventh Journal*, p. 57.

state of affairs at that time remains, among a great mass of similar evidence, in a pamphlet [1] published in 1641, almost exactly a hundred years previous to the days of which we are now speaking. This description introduces us to the similarly illiterate and incoherent leaderships in worship of "Greene the felt-maker, Martin the button-maker, Spencer the coachman, Rodgers the glover," and of various others, who claimed to speak "only as the Spirit moves," and who "for this one reason set themselves against those scholars, as bishops, deans, and deacons, who strive to construe the Scripture according to the translation of the Hebrew, Greek and Latin; which last language [because of its association with popery], stinks like a piece of bief a twelvemonth old."

A lively contemporaneous letter home to England gives an obviously not sympathetic, but, on the other hand, a probably not very much exaggerated, account of things in some places shortly after Mr. Whitefield's first transit through the colonies: [2] —

"There is a Creature here whom you perhaps never heard of before. It is called *an Exhorter*. It is of both Sexes, but generally of the Male, and young. Its distinguishing Qualities, are *Ignorance, Impudence, Zeal*. . . . Such of them as have good Voices do *great Execution;* they move their Hearers, make them cry, faint, swoon, fall into Convulsions. . . . The Ministers have generally

---

[1] *The Brownists Synagogue, or A Late Discovery of their Conventicles, etc.*

[2] *State of Religion in New England since the Reverend Mr. George Whitefield's Arrival there* [Glasgow, 1742], pp. 6, 7.

EXTRAVAGANCES. 97

endeavoured to preserve some kind of Order, and been satisfied with the crying out of a Number at the hearing of their Sermons; (the Minister that never made Somebody or other cry, is unconverted) but the Exhorters tarry in the Meeting-house with the People after the Minister is gone, and sometimes several of them exhort at once in different Parts of the House, and then there is terrible Doings. You may hear screaming, singing, laughing, praying, all at once; and, in other Parts, they fall into Visions, Trances, Convulsions. When they come out of their Trances, they commonly tell a senseless Story of Heaven and Hell, and whom and what they saw there."

This is not sympathetic, as was said, but neither can it be deemed untruthful. The evidence is authentic and multifarious that there prevailed very widely extravagances and disorders in the conduct of so-called religious meetings, of which the following from an eye-witness may be taken as an example: [1] —

"The Meeting was carried on with what appeared to me great Confusion; some *screaming* out in Distress and Anguish; some *praying;* others *singing;* some again *jumping up and down* the House, while others were *exhorting;* some *lying along* on the Floor, and others *walking* and *talking:* The whole with a very great Noise, to be heard at a *Mile's* Distance, and continued almost the whole Night. . . . Many of the *young Women* would go about the House *praying* and *exhorting;* then they would separate themselves from the other People, and

---

[1] Chauncy's *Seasonable Thoughts*, pp. 239, 40.

get into a Corner of the House to *sing* and *rejoice* together; And then they would break forth into *as great a Laughter as could be*, to think, as they exprest it, that they should go Hand in Hand to Heaven. . . . And all this, when, at the same Time, there were *threescore* Persons lying, some on the Floor, some across the Seats, while others were held up and supported in great Distress."

When so grave and distinguished a minister as Rev. Solomon Williams of Lebanon, Connecticut, felt compelled to preach and publish a sermon,[1] occasioned by the visions seen in a trance by two children, a boy of thirteen and a girl of eleven, wherein they alleged that they had been shown the Book of Life, and the names of some of their friends and neighbors written in it, but that the Book lacked only one page of being full, by which tidings the whole town of Lebanon was disquieted, — it is plain that attention was being turned and importance attached to accidental and even injurious circumstances attendant upon the awakening, and caused oftentimes by violent and ignorant leadership in it, to the serious detriment of its lasting good effects on the spiritual life.

The drawbacks on the benign character of the spiritual movement, occasioned by the extravagance of exhorters, the stress put upon visions, trances, impulses, and revelations, were indeed great. We need not go to the pages of Chauncy alone, who, for his " Seasonable Thoughts on the State of Religion in

---

[1] *The More Excellent Way*, Prefatory Letter [1742].

New England," was most unjustly stigmatized as an enemy of God and religion, for evidence on this point. Jonathan Edwards, the great supporter and historian of the movement, gives more than one third of his whole volume[1] on the Revival, to pointing out things in it which were to be "corrected and avoided." The witness of the ministerial associations of the period is very generally similar. Many of them felt compelled to put on record conclusions like those adopted by the Hartford North Association, August 11, 1741, of which it is sufficient to quote here from the manuscript record two only: —

"Whether any Weight is to be Laid upon those screachings, cryings out, faintings and convulsions which sometimes attend ye terrifying Language of some preachers and others, as Evidences of, or necessary to, a genuine Conviction of Sin, humiliation, and preparation for Christ? Agreed in the *Negative*, as also that there is no Weight to be Laid upon those Visions or visional Discoveries by some of Late pretended to, of Heaven or Hell, or ye body or blood of Christ, *viz* as represented to ye eyes of ye body.

"Whether ye assertion of some Itinerant preachers that ye pure Gospel and especially ye doctrines of Regeneration and Justification by faith are not preached in these Churches: their Rash censuring ye body of our clergy as Carnal and unconverted men, and notoriously unfit for their office is not such a sinfull and Scandalous violation of the fifth and ninth Commandments of ye Moral Law

---

[1] *Some Thoughts Concerning the Present Revival of Religion in New England* [1742], pp. 188-326.

as ought to be testified against? . . . Agreed in ye affirmative."

On the whole, it is not surprising that, before the second tour of Mr. Whitefield through New England, in 1744, extensive divisions of sentiment respecting the revivalistic movement, so largely represented by him, should have developed, and should practically have separated the ministry, as also the churches, into two parties. Formal legislation had been enacted in Connecticut[1] to suppress itineracy in that commonwealth, and several ministers and laymen had been imprisoned for preaching without leave in the parishes of settled ministers. The faculties of Harvard and Yale published "Testimonies" against "Mr. Whitefield and his conduct;" protests against his admission to the pulpits of the churches were adopted by several district ministerial associations in Massachusetts and Connecticut, and by the General Association of the latter colony. So that, though several of the Boston ministers still opened their pulpits to him, and it was even proposed to build there the largest church edifice in America for his permanent occupancy, Whitefield's second coming was attended by comparatively trifling results. Of his subsequent visitations to New England in 1754, 1764, and 1770, there is here no especial occasion to speak.

The great wave of emotion which rolled across the country in the Great Awakening years of 1740,

---

[1] *Colonial Records*, vol. viii. 456, 457.

1741, and 1742, subsided almost as rapidly as it arose. Additions to the churches rapidly declined. The year 1741 saw sixty-nine admissions to the Old South Church in Boston, and twenty-four in 1742; 1746 saw the number reduced to two; 1747 to six, and 1748 to three. At Northampton, where the interest attending the revival in 1740 was very intense, and where, as Mr. Edwards records,[1] "It was a *very frequent* Thing to see an *House-full of Outcries, Faintings, Convulsions,* and such like, both with *Distress* and also with *Admiration* and *Joy*," and where great numbers were added to the church, the interest so declined that, from 1744 to 1748, not a new candidate was propounded.

In Hartford, where more conservative methods prevailed, and where most of the ministers were under a bitter and false reproach as enemies to the Revival, something of the same difference was also manifested. Twenty-seven persons came into full communion in the First Church in 1741, against five in 1742, four in 1743, and one in 1744.

But, though, in some of its manifestations, the Great Awakening seemed ephemeral, there were characteristics of it and consequences flowing from it which profoundly affected the religious life, not only of the immediate period, but of much after-time.

Not only did it at once reinforce the membership of the New England churches by a large numerical accession, — the estimates are as wide apart as the reasonable one of ten or twelve thousand, and the

[1] *Christian History*, January 14, 1743.

absurd one of fifty thousand,— but the members so introduced came into the churches under the impulse of an intensity of feeling, and, in many cases, under the pressure of dogmatic convictions, to which the two or three generations of their predecessors had been comparative strangers. A great, and in some respects a lasting, effect had been wrought by those two or three years of unusual spiritual awakening, and by the activities accompanying them, upon the type of prevalent religious life.

One indication — which in its turn became also a cause — of this altered type of religious feeling is to be found in the changed character of preaching.

The accusations were, indeed, unjust which Whitefield and James Davenport in that heated time made against the New England ministry, that they were mostly unconverted men and preachers of a lifeless Gospel. Gilbert Tennent's characterization of them[1] as "blind and dead men," "drones," "dupes," "men whom the devil drives into the ministry," may be left to the contempt its extravagant censoriousness deserves. But it is not to be denied that the Awakening produced a mighty change in the pulpit spirit throughout New England. It was not for nothing, however many of the ministers dissented from the methods of Mr. Whitefield, that that fiery evangelist had swept across their orbit of vision, and that his preaching had been so potent in stirring the hearts of men. Even the response of the multitude to the

[1] In his Sermon dedicated to the people of Nottingham, Pennsylvania.

harangues of ignorant exhorters had its lessons for such of the ministers as were wise. And among the preachers of the Awakening hour, and of following years, there were some of eminent gifts, whose piety could not be questioned, whose methods could not be substantially condemned, and whose influence was propagative and contagious. Edwards, Parsons, Mills, Wheelock, Pomeroy, and, as a man of pulpit power greater than any of them, Joseph Bellamy, were all enthusiastically engaged in the revival movement in its most active stage, and abated none of their earnestness afterward. The effect of the awakening, and of the examples of its chief promoters, could not but be felt in the pulpits generally. Even in communities like some in Connecticut, where the ministers were thought inimical to the revival, there is ample recorded evidence of greatly increased ministerial activity; of heightened fervency of appeal from the pulpit; of multiplied occasions of public and social worship, and enhanced pastoral vigilance. The pulpits of the country were revived, and more lastingly than the pews.

As a natural accompaniment of this more strenuous presentation of religious truth, religious experience took on, all through the immediate years which we call those of the Awakening, and sporadically and occasionally long afterward, an intensity of character, especially in its outward manifestation, that had been unprecedented in previous New England history. The extensive prevalence of physical phenomena, of swoonings, trances, outcries, and convulsions, has already been pointed out. Even so great and clear-sighted a man as Jonathan Edwards pronounced these manifestations,[1] if "not certain," yet "probable tokens of God's presence, and arguments of the success of preaching." He felt called on to "rejoice in them, and to bless God for them." And it is worth while to note that their place and value in religious experience became the subject of large discussion; careful arguments in their behalf, like those of Mr. Edwards's, being made by many. These arguments found, naturally, welcome response in the minds of people sympathetically inclined toward the revival itself. On the other hand, a considerable body of antagonistic literature remains to us, embracing resolutions passed by ministerial associations, sermons deprecating such manifestations and impeaching their utility, and even republished pamphlets from abroad setting forth the alleged misleading and dangerous character of such phenomena, as illustrated in other lands, — all witnessing to the interest felt in a phase of religious experience at once so prevalent, so intense, and so obscure.

Mr. Edwards himself might easily be excused — if any excuse be thought necessary — for the leniency of his opinion about these physical phenomena, in view of their wonderful manifestation in his own house at various earlier times, and especially in 1742, in the person of his beautiful and saintly wife, Sarah Pierpont, whose "faintings," "loss of strength," "sinkings down to the floor," repeated for many

[1] *Thoughts on the Revival*, p. 192.

successive days, she distinctly ascribes — and he as devoutly records as only to be ascribed — to disclosures of heavenly things, and influxes of spiritual influence too great for mortal flesh to endure.[1]

But, account for these things as we may, they were a feature of the spiritual phenomena of the period, more marked and pervasive than they have been at any other time in New England history: albeit they have, to some extent and in lessened degree, appeared and re-appeared in many subsequent seasons of religious interest down to our own day.

Closely connected with what has just been spoken of, and probably in part at least psychologically explanatory of it, was that feature of the religious life of the revival epoch which consisted in a greatly vivified sense of the pressure on men's minds of certain dogmatic views of religious truth; especially those of the Divine sovereignty and holiness, and of human dependence and sinfulness.

In both of these respects there was, in point of fact, a distinct reversion of experience to an earlier type; to that of a century and more previous. We are very strongly reminded by the narratives of spiritual struggle which have been preserved to us from this Great Awakening era, under the preachings of Whitefield, Edwards, and Tennent, of those earlier struggles which were connected with the utterances of Perkins and Rogers in Old England, and their disciples, Hooker and Shepherd, in New England.

[1] See Dwight's *Life of Edwards*, chapter xiv., and Edwards's *Thoughts on the Revival*, pp. 62-78.

Indeed, there was such a correspondency of moral and spiritual conditions between the two epochs, across the breadth of the century between, that many books published in the former era were now republished as suited to present needs,— for example, Hooker's "Poor Doubting Christian Drawne unto Christ," first printed in London in 1629, and now reprinted at Boston in 1743; or Shepherd's "Sincere Convert" and "Sound Beleever," first published in 1645 and 1646, and again reprinted, both of them, in 1742.

There was a certain perceivable difference, nevertheless, which cannot fail to strike the careful reader, in the methods of setting forth the same tremendous facts — say of sovereignty and dependence, of holiness and sinfulness — in the two periods, which must, to some extent, have modified the experiences to which the strong assertion of these facts gave rise. That is to say, there was in the earlier period much more of contentment with the vivid announcement and illustration of any alleged truth under consideration, and much less of an attempt to explain the truth and set it in its proper intellectual place as a thing to be rationally justified, than in the latter.

Take, for an example of what is thus perceivable, the treatment of the question of sinfulness, as this awful fact of human experience is handled by Thomas Hooker in 1632, and by Jonathan Edwards about 1740. Mr. Hooker says:[1] —

[1] *Soules Preparation* [1635], pp. 20-26.

"It is not every sight of sinne will serve the turne, nor every apprehension of a mans vilenesse. . . . Wee must looke on the nature of sinne in the venome of it, the deadly hurtfull nature that it hath, for plagues and miseries, it doth procure to our soules, and that you may doe . . . if you compare it with other things . . . that are most fearefull and horrible; As suppose any soule here present were to behold the damned in hell, and if the Lord should give thee a little peepe-hole into hell, that thou didst see the horror of those damned soules . . . then propound this to thy owne heart, what paines the damned in hell doe endure for sinne, . . . the least sinne that ever thou didst commit, though thou makest a light matter of it, is a greater evill then the paines of the damned in hell, setting aside their sinne; all the torments in hell are not so great an evill as the least sin is."

There you have a brief specimen of Mr. Hooker's method, — statement, illustration, intense even dramatic setting forth of the alleged fact; no attempt at all at showing why sin is sinful.

Mr. Edwards's language respecting sin is certainly not less expressive of the profoundest sense of its reality and dreadfulness: —

"My wickedness, as I am in myself," he says,[1] "has long appeared to me perfectly ineffable, swallowing up all thought and imagination . . . I know not how better to express what my sins appear to me to be, than by heaping infinite upon infinite, and multiplying infinite by

[1] *Personal Narrative*, Dwight's Life, p. 134.

infinite . . . When I look into my heart, and take a view of my wickedness, it looks like an abyss infinitely deeper than hell."

But Edwards was not content to have his hearers rest in mere belief and feeling of what he regarded as a fact. He must try to have them justify the fact to their own minds, and set it in its proper place in a more or less complete intellectual system. And therefore he, and many with and after him, undertook to explain the infinite evil and indesert of sin by "its being committed against an infinite object."[1] As God is an infinite being, sin against God must be an infinite sin. We most of us, probably, may think the elaborate argument, by which the great and acute intellect of Edwards attempted thus to prove to his hearers the evil of sin, is really only a trick of the imagination and a bit of word-play; but it shows the difference spoken of between the popular treatment of the same fact in 1740 and a century earlier.

A similar token of the difference referred to is to be seen in the unlike manner in which another point of spiritual experience was treated in the two eras. It has been seen[2] that Shepherd and Hooker both taught, in the first half of the seventeenth century, the doctrine of an unconditional submission to the divine will, so extreme as to involve a willingness to be lost. Hooker calls such a contentment in damnation a "blessed frame of heart." "O this heart is

[1] *Works* [1809], vii. 27, 28.
[2] *Ante*, p. 28.

worth Gold," he says.[1] But he does not undertake — beyond a mere reference to the indesert of the soul for anything better — to explain why such extremity of submission is obligatory or commendable.

But when, in 1740 and in subsequent years, there was a recrudescence of this extreme and — to most minds — harassing test of spiritual experience, the matter was stated in a very different way. When the fervid Sarah Edwards contemplated the possibility that it would be "most for the honour of God" that she should "die in horror" and live forever in torment, the ground of her "sweet quietness and alacrity of soul in consenting that it should be so," to the "banishing of all reluctance" even, was precisely that God would, in that case, be most glorified; and that God's glory was the creature's supreme duty.[2] When the cool and clear-headed Samuel Hopkins, a little later, took up and inculcated the same doctrine of an unconditional submission to the will of God, reaching even to a willingness to be eternally lost if it was for the highest glory of God and the good of the universe, he found the reason for its binding obligation in the duty of disinterested benevolence and willing acceptance of whatever would make for the largest welfare.[3]

All which suggests, what was indeed the fact, that New England thought, long comparatively indifferent to theology as a systematic subject of inquiry, was,

[1] *Humiliation*, pp. 106, 107.
[2] Dwight's *Life*, p. 182; *Thoughts*, p. 71.
[3] *Works* [1811], i. 465-491.

under the strong impulse of the Revival, awakening to a new interest in doctrinal matters. Questions were started in the hot hours of spiritual struggle which needed to be thought out in more leisurely days; questions of the extent and nature of man's ability under such appeals of the Gospel as had characterized that evangelistic time; questions of the relation of the divine promises to men in the condition in which the Awakening found or left them; questions of the nature of that process through which so many of the hopeful subjects of the Revival had passed; or of those moral attitudes and qualities that God requires of men always.

Such questions as these, together with the agitated but still unsettled problem of a proper theory of church relationship — of baptism and covenant, and sacramental privilege — were pressing with a new interest on the quickened mind of the period.

Thought was turning into the channel of systematic doctrine. A characteristic New England Theology was in the process of generation. And perhaps — aside, of course, from the momentous question of the bearing of revival experiences on the history of individual souls — the most important result of the Great Awakening was in the dogmatic discussions aroused by it, which ultimately worked themselves out, through the teachings of the two Edwardses, Bellamy, Hopkins, Emmons, and Dwight, into the general type of religious belief which is known as "New England Theology." This substantially harmonious though progressive movement was paralleled, however, on two sides,— on the one side, in the interest of an older orthodoxy, by the teachings of a conservative school, of diminishing numbers and declining influence, of which such men as Samuel Phillips, Thomas Clap, William Hart, and Moses Hemmenway may be taken as representatives; and on the other, by a liberalizing school, represented by Experience and Jonathan Mayhew, Charles Chauncy, Lemuel Briant, Samuel Webster, and Clark Brown, which ultimately developed into the Unitarianism of Channing and Ware, and the schism of the first part of the present century. But, as there has been occasion more than once previously to remark, doctrinal discussions, as such, do not come within the scope of our present design, and they are referred to now only as one of the factors influencing the religious life of the period.

In this aspect of them, these discussions undoubtedly tended very considerably to distract attention from individual spiritual concerns, and were among the causes of the subsidence of that form and degree of religious enthusiasm which had been so hailed by Edwards and his associates as the harbinger, almost, of a millennial day. And when to these polemic controversies was added the rigorous exercise of ecclesiastical measures, especially in Connecticut, for the repression of the more characteristic features of the Revival,— itineracy, lay-exhortation, and criticism of religious authority generally; and to these, again, the political agitation of a succession of French and Spanish wars which brought the conflicts of the

Old World to every New England door, it is not to be wondered at that the vision of the "Heaven upon Earth" which Edwards[1] seemed to behold as hopefully close at hand should have been dissipated as the rainbow is brushed by the gathering darkness from the sunset skies.

So rapid, indeed, was this change of happy prospect that, in 1758, only seventeen years after the Revival was in full progress, Rev. Benjamin Throop, in the Election Sermon preached before the Connecticut governor and legislature, felt compelled to say, in language strikingly indicative, not only of the spiritual declension, but of the doctrinal confusion of the time: —

"There is an awful Decay of Religion, and an unreasonable Spirit of Jealousy prevailing: the fear of God is amazingly cast off in this day. While some are disputing the Personality of the Godhead, and denying the Lord that bought them; others are ridiculing the important Doctrine of Atonement, and casting contempt upon the efficacious Merits of a Glorious Redeemer; many are exploding the Doctrine of a free and Sovereign Grace, and exalting humane Nature under all its Depravity to a situation equal to all its Necessities; thereby perverting the Designs of the Gospel, and frustrating, as far as may be, the Means of our Salvation."

There was, however, in certain quarters, a kind of one-sided prolongation of the Revival impulse to which entire justice has not been done by most nar-

[1] *Thoughts*, p. 149.

THE SEPARATISTS. 113

rators of our New England religious story. This was to be found among that scattered and imperfectly coördinated body of Christian people known as "Separatists." The story of Separatism in the period now under review is an obscure one. It is so partly because of the ephemeral character of the movement itself, and the perishing to a great extent of the documents whose preservation might have illustrated it; and partly because of the humble and illiterate quality of those mainly engaged in it.

They were men and women chiefly ignorant, enthusiastic, sensitive to the more emotional and accidental features of the Revival, and without intellectual or educational ballast to prevent their falling into easy confusion and error. But there is something to be said for them, nevertheless. It should be remembered as one explanation of the whole Separatist endeavor, that almost all the regular churches of the period were under the operation of the Half-way Covenant, which brought into membership — at least into partial membership — admittedly unconverted persons. In Connecticut, furthermore, the churches were under the control of a legal system which established a State Religion as truly as in England or in Spain. Both these facts were obnoxious to the Separatists. They believed, as did the first fathers of New England, that a church should consist of regenerate persons only; and that Christ alone, and not any civil power, was the head and fountain of all authority in the Church. In both these convictions we certainly must sympathize with them, as against the churches and the civil powers arrayed in opposition to them.

But the Separatists also held the belief that the discernment of regenerate persons — of whom only a church ought to be composed — was a power given, not alone to apostles and prophets of the primitive age, but intrusted to the church in perpetuity for its habitual guidance and defense. They believed that, by the employment of the "Key of Knowledge" granted them by Christ, a Christian could be as well distinguished from a non-Christian "as a sheep from a dog." The test of fellowship was the "inward actings of their own souls," moving toward or recoiling from sympathy with those brought into association with them.

Joined with this persuasion of direct illumination in discerning the spirits of men, was the further belief that the Holy Spirit's guidance was sufficient for all religious instruction, superseding the necessity of "book-learning" or even of careful preparation in "preaching the word." This was doubtless an honest conviction, but it was certainly a very convenient one, for they had almost no persons of superior cultivation among them. Naturally they fell under the guidance of well-nigh illiterate instructors, taken from their own lay membership, and ordained as their ministers. Persuaded — and often rightly persuaded — of the sadly secularized character of the churches with which they had been connected, they separated from them and established churches of their own.

THE SEPARATISTS. 115

Their numbers were never very large, though more than thirty organizations in more or less complete church-estate existed in Connecticut alone; the best known of which were at Canterbury, New London, Norwich, Preston, Plainfield, Lyme, Middletown, Windsor, and Suffield. They were imperfectly associated in what they called " The Convention of the Confederated Strict Congregational Churches." They maintained ecclesiastical intercourse with similar churches by way of council in Massachusetts and Rhode Island, and, to some extent, in New York, New Hampshire, New Jersey, and Pennsylvania.

The number of such churches in Massachusetts is uncertain, but the best known among them were those of Attleboro', Rehoboth, Middleboro', Bridgewater, Grafton, Sunderland, Norton, Wrentham, Charlestown, and Sturbridge.

Everywhere, as come-outers from the " standing-order," and as being on the whole a humble sort of folk, the tribulations of these Separating brethren were severe. In Connecticut their disabilities and trials were really arduous. Calling themselves Congregationalists, and, indeed, standing on the original Cambridge Platform of Congregationalism, they could not secure, as Baptist or Episcopal dissenters could, exemption from taxation for the support of the churches from which they seceded, and were often subjected to distraint of their property, and sometimes to imprisonment of their persons, for delinquency in paying legal dues to churches they had renounced; or for preaching or exhorting within the bounds of parishes belonging by ecclesiastical and civil arrangement to other men. Rev. Elisha Paine, once a lawyer of considerable repute in Connecticut, but afterward perhaps the leading minister in the Separatist connection, who died in good old age and honor as pastor of a church on Long Island, was imprisoned once in Worcester, Massachusetts, and several times in Connecticut, for preaching in other minister's bounds, and his property was again and again attached, and portions of it confiscated, for non-payment of taxes to the regular ministry.

There can be no doubt that the original impelling impulse of the Separatist movement was, in the main, a devout and sincere one. It was an endeavor after a more fervid type of piety, and more activity in the church-membership, than the Separatist brethren thought possible in the mixed fellowship of a " standing-order " presided over by a State-authorized ministry. One is tempted to drop a tear over the failure of anticipations which had in them so much of good intent. For of course they could but fail. The good in them was over-weighted with too much of what was not good to make success possible.

Their doctrine of the non-necessity of education and the sufficiency of immediate spiritual insight secured to them an ignorant ministry, running off not infrequently into a ranting and fanatic one. Their belief that they could infallibly judge of the spiritual qualifications for membership in their churches, and that the test of such fitness was " the inward actions of their own souls," was not only productive of measureless mistake in the admission of people to their fellowship, but was even more destructive to peace among themselves afterward. Absolute knowledge of one another's good estate at entrance to the church did not prevent equally positive doubt about it very soon after.

Mutual criticism, censoriousness, and the extravagant employment of church discipline tore their churches in sunder. The few annals which remain are largely annals of councils called to adjust quarrels based on alleged injustices done by purgative processes among members who once infallibly knew each other to be "saints," as they were habituated to call themselves.

Accustomed to the fervors of a hortatory style of address, whose imagery, in default of other sources, was largely borrowed from the Bible, their preaching, and even their official documents, took on a kind of Apocalyptic strain which reminds us of the days of the Roundheads and Fifth-Monarchy men in the times of the English Commonwealth. A few extracts from manuscripts of official character in this ecclesiastical connection, hitherto unpublished, may give the flavor of many others.

Rev. Samuel Drown, who had been apparently conducting an evangelistic meeting in Providence in June, 1752, writes to the Canterbury Church: —

"I have been Laboring within these few Days in providence Church to bring about the Kingdom to the

House of David but could not affect the work alone . . . wherefore I intreet you to Gird up your Liens and Cry to god to Leed you to the Choice of faithful Brethren and send them by the order of the holy Ghost, every man with his sword girt upon his thy, for such a battel is coming as you have scarcly fought here to fore."

Enfield Church, in tribulation because of a case of discipline, sends out its call for a council in these terms, in May, 1753 : —

" May the God of Zion give you to hear ye Grones of this Part of Zion under her Present Standing, for we are under Broken Surcumstances, Divided into two Parties. Zion here is in distress ; the Church Sore Broken in the Place of Dragons . . . therefore do we cry to you as Gods witnesses for help."

The church of Charlestown, divided between two candidates for its pulpit, calls for the advice of its sister churches in this way : —

" April 26, 1752. Dear Brethren We are Wading through many Tribulations Toward the Blissfull Shores of Eternal Day where we Shant Stand in Need of Councils to Inlighten and Direct us into the True worship and Discipline of the House of God. Neither shall we stand in Need of your Witness to Direct us in the Choice of a Pastor. But O Dear Brethren we are in the Militant State and Stand in Need of your help in all These. Therefore our Cry to our God and to you his Witnesses ; Help, help, help, . . . ye Battle goes hard on the side of the Faithfull ; therefore again we Cry Gird on your Sword, Mount the White Horses, and Come forth to the help of the Lord against the Mighty; and as you hear the Trumpet sound on this part of Zion's walls, the Certain Sound is, *viz.* We have been in Search of a Pastor till many of us is Lost in the Wilderness; for our Evidences Cross each other, some for James Simon and some for Sam!! Niles. The grace of our Lord Jesus Christ be with you. Amen."

"Our Evidences cross each other;" yes, that was often the trouble with the Separatist people.

One more quotation only, which has a kind of pathetic side to it, in spite of its peculiarity. Sister Hannah Watts, apparently visiting in Boston in January, 1748, writes home to the Connecticut church of which she was a member: —

"I am astonished. I am astonished. O amazing, amazing, amazing. Who do you think that it is that is writing to Saints, calling them brethren in Christ Jesus. why i will tell you who it is it is the very scrapings of the bottom of hell O wonderfull wonderfull i must tell you how my redemtion looks to me. Methinks i see that blessed redeemer when he had brought up all the rest of the elect out of hell he missed one he could not rest no but down go again and scrapes the very bottom and hottest place in all hell to bring up this hell monster O how unsearchable is that love."

There can be no doubt that Hannah Watts was an excellent woman; and the experience she was conscious of did not differ very much from that which Edwards had, when he wrote in words quoted a little while ago: "Infinite upon infinite . . . Infinitely deeper than hell." But it may be questioned, nevertheless, whether Hannah Watts's letter, read in church-meeting, tended much to edification.

More space has been given to this Separatist movement and to these Separatist utterances than perhaps seems proportionate to the subject, but it has been given intentionally, and for two reasons. One is, that the Separatist endeavor was, in one aspect of it, a direct outcome of the Revival, and, indeed, a kind of prolongation of some of its most characteristic features; the other reason is, that treatment of the subject itself has been comparatively infrequent, and even the materials for its treatment relatively scanty. The subject deserves a fuller investigation than it has ever yet received.

With the gradual disuse of the Half-way Covenant which began to follow, slowly indeed, the discussions of Edwards and Bellamy, and of others later in the last century, one main principle which the Separatist churches stood for no longer retained significance. Some of them returned to communion with the churches from which they came out. A few of them — like the Second Church in Middletown, Connecticut, which still retains the name of "The Church in the Strict Congregational Society," — developed into strong churches in connection with the general Congregational fellowship. A few passed over into the Baptist communion, toward which, indeed, their doctrine of an exclusively regenerate membership, as set over against a membership at least in part based on baptism in infancy, rather naturally led them. Perhaps the larger number of them gradually died out; some of them in more or less of confusion, scandal, and smoke.

So ended a chapter of religious life which had in it a good deal of the pathetic and not a little of the good, mingled with much that is of a less noble or interesting kind; a chapter which still awaits its proper treatment at the hands of some painstaking and sympathetic historian.

The closing years of the period under review in this lecture beheld the introduction into New England of another religious agency — that of Methodism — itself the direct outcome of the English revival impulse of which the Great Awakening was the American counterpart. New England Methodism had, indeed, no direct connection with the Separatist movement just described; but, like that a child of the new religious quickening, it shared with Separatism its fervor in worship and in hortatory appeal; while the strongly-knit organization impressed upon it by its founder guarded Methodism from the excesses in which Separatism made shipwreck. Established in New York in 1766, its seeds were unsuccessfully planted in Boston in 1772; the short-lived congregation there gathered being scattered by the turmoil of the Revolutionary War. The permanent introduction of Methodism into New England was the work of the indefatigable Rev. Jesse Lee, whose first class-meeting was formed within the borders of Fairfield, Connecticut, in September, 1789; and was followed, through Lee's efforts, before the close of 1792, by similar organizations in each of the New England states. Once firmly established in New England, Methodism rapidly became a considerable, and ultimately a most important, factor in the religious life of the region, though that development belongs chronologically to an epoch subsequent to the one included in the present lecture.

Our fathers of the "Standing Order" looked with scant favor on the Methodist beginnings. Their strong Calvinism viewed the Arminianism of the movement with hostility, their comparatively unemotional conceptions of the proprieties of worship had little sympathy with the unconventionality of Methodist services. As late as 1800, the Hartford North Association, for example, voted unanimously that it was "not consistent to dismiss and recommend the members of our churches to the Methodists." But the seed thus sown at the close of the period now under review was destined to bear much fruit.

It was a distinct gain to our New England religious life, however unwelcome to the strict Calvinists of our eighteenth and early nineteenth century churches, that the Methodists contributed in presenting a type of Arminianism which was also fervid and evangelistic. Jonathan Edwards had been moved to preach the sermons which were the immediate human cause of the spiritual awakening of 1734 and 1735, at Northampton, by reason of the spread of "Arminian" views; and New England controversialists, throughout the period of the Great Awakening, made much use of the term in the charges and counter-charges of theologic debate. But the "Arminianism" which New England had known was cold, unemotional, chiefly marked by a negative attitude toward the sharper doctrines of Calvinism, by an exaltation of the salvatory value of human virtue, and by an unspiritual formalism in worship. With the Methodist advent New England was compelled, rather reluctantly, to recognize that there was an Arminianism possible which was no less aggressively revivalistic in method, evangelical in spirit, and high-wrought in feeling than Edwardean Calvinism itself.

It was advantageous, also, to the spiritual development of New England that a religious organization should be introduced within its borders, which gave to the layman more opportunity for utterance, and for public testimony to religious experiences at other times beside his entrance into churchmembership, than the Congregational churches of the last century afforded. A change was to come, indeed, with the beginning of the Evangelical Reawakening which will constitute the theme of the next lecture: the prayer meeting and the Sunday school were to be taken into the service of the Congregational churches; but, in the period now under review, any form of worship in which other voice was heard than that of the pastor was rare. The Methodist exhorter and the Methodist class-meeting met a spiritual want which our churches did not then wholly satisfy.

Nor can it be denied that there was room in New England for a more hortatory and emotional form of worship than Congregationalism has always offered. The Separatist movement showed clearly that there were not a few who preferred the stirring addresses and fervent prayers of enthusiastic men, even though uneducated, to the more formal and elaborate services, and the carefully prepared sermons, which Congregationalism deemed suited to the dignity of its worship. That desire Methodism met successfully where Separatism failed; and the gain to New England spiritual life has been permanent. But these advantages were mostly still in the future, when the period now under contemplation closed. The beginnings only of Methodism had been made, and its influence was as yet inconspicuous.

The general period of religious affairs in New England which has occupied attention in the present lecture terminated very differently from the way in which it commenced.

Beginning in a burst of spiritual activity which seemed, to use a phrase already quoted from its greatest representative, likely to "make New England a kind of Heaven upon Earth," it ended in comparative coldness and torpidity in the religious life. The distractions of doctrinal controversy, the acrimonies of ecclesiastical strife, and the anxieties of political conflict reaching forward and culminating in the Revolutionary War and the establishment of the Federal Government, diverted attention from those considerations of supreme personal religious concern which so occupied this period's opening days.

However, let us not underestimate the benefit of that pungent early experience, or too darkly judge the character of the years which followed. Certain things had been accomplished which, in a large consideration of religious welfares, were of abiding value. The churches had not only been reinforced by very great accessions through the Revival, but to a considerable extent they had been purified. Blows, not immediately fatal, indeed, but destined to be fatal, to the disastrous Half-way-Covenant system of church-membership had been struck; and the minds of men were fast opening to the evils which that system entailed. Signs of its approaching dissolution were multiplying. And besides this, in spite of the evils which doctrinal controversy always occasions, there were a discipline and an education in the close handling of religious truth attendant upon the powerful discussions of the great themes of religious thought from Edwards to Dwight, from Clap to Hemmenway, from Chauncy to Brown, which gave augury that when New England should be stirred again by spiritual impulses from above, the results might be expected to be more intelligent, more abiding, and, in some respects, certainly more beneficent than any ever before experienced in the land. Such results were realized. It will be the object of the next lecture to tell in what way.

IV.

THE EVANGELICAL REAWAKENING.

It was mentioned in the preceding lecture that the period stretching from the Great Awakening onward nearly to the close of the eighteenth century, was a time of comparative formality and deadness in the religious life of the people and churches of New England.

Certain contributory causes, — like the reaction of men's feelings from the excesses of the Whitefieldian excitement; the prevalence of ecclesiastical controversy; colonial and revolutionary warfare; and the strife of political antagonism attendant upon and following the establishment of the Federal Constitution, — were pointed out as among the more recognizable of the apparent influences which produced the prevalent indifference of men's minds to the distinctly personal aspects of religious truth and duty.

From this condition of declension the religious life of New England was destined to revive most powerfully in the period under survey in this lecture. Much more than in the era called the "Great Awakening," was a profound and fruitful spiritual vivification to move on men's minds and character.

DOCTRINAL PARTIES.

But, to understand the special quality and the guiding influences of this reawakening era of New England's religious life, it will be needful to take at least a hasty glance at the state of doctrinal belief in this period, and at the different positions of theological parties.

It has been seen that during the period from 1735 to about 1790, theology was taking on more exact statement, under the leadership of a series of strenuous and powerful thinkers; and, in spite of much spiritual indifference, was getting a closer grasp on the intellect of the average hearer of the preaching of that time. This theological thinking had taken three main lines.

There was in that period, as has already been briefly noted, what, for want of a better name, may be called a Liberalizing Movement of thought, under the lead of such men as Chauncy, Mayhew, Briant, Webster, and Brown. As yet the tendency of this school, which was destined to lead on to fully developed Unitarianism, was not perhaps distinctly recognized by its promoters, — certainly was not openly avowed. The more immediate points of contrast between the teachings of this class of able and cultivated men and those of the New England preachers generally, were the diminished emphasis put by them on the necessity and merits of Christ's sacrifice as a ground of men's spiritual hope, and the heightened emphasis placed on virtuous character as the most important element in the conditions of acceptance with God. This general school of thought was, however, as yet comparatively small, and was chiefly confined to eastern Massachusetts. It did not very seriously affect the processes of New England's religious life till the dawn of the nineteenth century.

Much more influential, by weight of numbers and of historical prestige, was a second general school of theologians who may properly be called Old-Calvinists. They adhered to the historically orthodox views of the New England fathers concerning the sovereignty of God, the inherited and imputed depravity of man, the arbitrariness and practical irresistibility of grace; but they believed — and taught also — that, though grace was sovereign in its bestowments, and could neither be purchased nor commanded, it was, nevertheless, generally imparted in connection with the use of "means" employed by the subject of it; as, by his prayers, his reading of Scripture, his attendance on the preaching of God's house. Such means, honestly employed, put men in a favorable way for obtaining the more special and effectual bestowments of divine help essential to salvation. And, though men could not of themselves make certain the result, they could make it vastly more probable; because, though grace itself was not within their power, the employment of the appointed means of grace certainly was; and such employment was not only hopeful as to the accomplishment of its object in procuring the ultimate gift of saving grace, but it rendered men less guilty, while they thus made use of the means, than they would be in their neglect. The "Old-Calvinist"

THE OLD-CALVINISTS.

position was well expressed by Rev. Samuel Phillips of Andover, Massachusetts, when he says:[1] —

"I can't suppose, that any one . . . who at all Times, faithfully improves the *common Grace* he has, *that is to say*, is diligent in attending on the appointed Means of Grace, with a Desire to profit thereby; . . . and in a Word, who walks up to his Light, to the utmost of his Power, shall perish for want of *special* and saving Grace."

Similarly, at a considerably later period, Rev. Moses Hemmenway said,[2] of the "Old-Calvinist" position in regard to such duties as prayer, reading of the Bible, and meditation on the soul's needs, which Hopkinsians stigmatized as useless and dangerous unregenerate doings: —

"In general, our observance of these duties is required as the ordinary method and means, whereby God is pleased to prepare a sinner for, and then communicate to him that saving grace, light and life, whereby he becomes a new creature, and is enabled and disposed unto those exercises and acts which are spiritually good, and with which, according to the gospel promises, eternal life is connected."

Inculcations to the employment of the means of grace were therefore legitimate, and were a proper and most indispensable part of the pastoral function.

The Old-Calvinist party was eminently respectable both by reason of numbers and character. Its

---

[1] *Orthodox Christian* (1738), p. 75.
[2] Hemmenway's *Seven Sermons* (1767), p. 46.

members were distributed extensively through New England, though preponderatingly more in relative proportion in the northern and eastern than in the southern and western parts. These latter sections of territory, though not without their able representatives of the older type of theologians just spoken of, were more especially under the influence of a third class of New England divines, now briefly to be referred to.

This third school of theologians embraced the representatives of what was more or less opprobriously called "New Light," or "New-Divinity." They traced their doctrinal lineage from Edwards, through Bellamy, Hopkins, West, and Smalley. Not altogether at agreement among themselves in subordinate points of speculation, they were substantially one in the main outlines of their conception and support of religious faith. The ablest of these successors of Edwards, and the man who most powerfully stamped the impress of his own intellectual convictions and his moral sentiments on his associates and successors, was Samuel Hopkins. With small modifications, his positions may be taken as the representative positions of the New-Divinity in the period under consideration in the present lecture.

The sovereignty of God was never so affirmed — speaking now, of course, of New England history — as by the teachers of this party. It was a sovereignty which reached not only to the guidance and control, but to the ultimate causation, of all events and acts, even of sin itself. Yet sin lies not in the cause, but in the act; hence it was believed that the honor of God was preserved safe, while man was infinitely guilty. Man's guilt, furthermore, is his own in the sense that he is not merely the actual, but the sole, author of it, — the Old-Calvinist theory of an inherited or imputed sinfulness being abandoned by these theologians.

The essential quality of sin is selfishness. Every man at bottom is totally selfish, and therefore totally depraved. All operations of a human soul previous to its supernatural regeneration — even those operations seemingly most disinterested and beneficent — are really resolvable into some form of self-love, and are therefore wholly malignant and sinful. Seeking salvation, even, from any other than a disinterested motive is simply, as Thomas Shepherd had declared it a hundred and fifty years before, one of the " nine easie wayes . . . all which lead to hell." [1]

The essential quality of holiness, on the other hand, is benevolence. God is infinitely benevolent, and so infinitely holy. The test of all holiness is benevolence, or love to being in general, and to all particular beings in proportion to the amount of being each possesses. Hence a proper criterion of all true piety is a willing submission to the disposal of the Infinite Possessor of infinite being.

Nothing short of this unconditional submission is an act acceptable to God, for anything short of this is selfishness, and therefore sin. " Means of grace,"

[1] *Sincere Convert*, pp. 154, 160.

therefore, in the Old-Calvinist sense, there are none. To exhort men to the use of "means" is to fix their attention on adventitious and even misleading and deceiving matters, when the one only and instant obligation of the sinner is unconditional submission to the divine will. Indeed, the use of means is not merely idle, but criminal. As Hopkins phrases it :[1] —

"Awakened, convinced sinners, with whom most means are used, and who are most attentive to the concerns of their souls, and most in earnest in the use of means, are commonly, if not always, really more guilty and odious in God's sight than they who are secure and at ease in their sins."

Or as Emmons says :[2] —

"The best desires and prayers of sinners [are] altogether selfish, criminal and displeasing to God."

Nothing is pleasing but instant submission, instant exercise of disinterested and universal benevolence. And this man has natural power to do; but no moral power. He can if he will; but he cannot make himself will. Only the immediate interposition of Infinite Power, in pursuance of an elective determination, can do that. Guilty, — all the more sinful for every moment's use of so-called religious endeavor, short of the naturally possible but morally impossible act of self-renunciation whose exercise itself implies a change of heart, — his only hope is in

---

[1] *Use of Means* (1765), p. 125.
[2] *Autobiography*, Works, vol. i., xii.

an interposition not only of divine, but of irresistible, grace.[1]

The representatives of these three general types of religious belief in New England were all personally devout and sincere men; but it cannot be doubted that aggressiveness and zeal, and perhaps the larger measure of intellectual ability also, were on the side of the third, or New-Divinity, advocates. These were also often called Hopkinsians, from the name of the most resolute setter-forth of their distinctive peculiarities; and sometimes still again, "Berkshire Divinity men," from the residence successively at Stockbridge of two chief champions of the party, and the proximity to them of other adherents of their views. Representatives of this school of thought were largely also Yale College men; and in Connecticut they came to be much in a majority in the ministry. They were substantially harmonious, mutually supporting, and enthusiastic in their convictions; and they were animated not only by the stimulus of a certain newness in their characteristic presentations of religious truth, but also, as they thought, by the possession of positive advantages in escaping from dilemmas and inconsistencies attendant on positions different from their own. It was in a self-congratulating apprehension of these advantages, when compared with their brethren

---

[1] "Common grace is granted to all who enjoy the light of the gospel, while special grace is granted to none but the elect. . . . Special grace is always irresistible." Emmons, *Works* (1842), v. 105.

of the "Old-Calvinist" party, that they sometimes called themselves "Consistent-Calvinists."

When, therefore, about the year 1797, after a long period of comparative insensibility, there swept over the land one of those profound and pervasive emotional stirrings, whose mysterious approach and whose lasting personal results devout men of all times ascribe to the direct agency of God's Spirit, it was perfectly inevitable, in the then existing state of New England thought, that the revival should take on a distinctly dogmatic character; and that, more narrowly still, it should also to a very great extent be a New-Divinity revival. Not, indeed, that its scope and effects were measured and limited by the boundaries of New-Divinity teachings. It would have been suspiciously against the doctrine of Divine Sovereignty, which Consistent-Calvinists so strenuously insisted on, had that been the case. But, after all, account for it as we may, there can be no question that, speaking in a large and general sense, and recognizing very considerable limitations to the statement, the revival period which began in 1797, and which was followed at various epochs by similar awakenings for over forty years, was conspicuously Hopkinsian in character, and illustrative in experience of what might be anticipated as the results of that system of doctrine.

The revival itself was widespread. Most powerful perhaps — certainly in its earlier stages — in Connecticut, it reached extensively through Massachusetts, Vermont, and New Hampshire. It took hold

CHARACTER OF THE REVIVAL. 135

not on Congregational churches alone, but on the Baptist churches as far down the eastern coast as Penobscot Bay. Nor did it pass by entirely unmoved even those congregations in Boston and near vicinity whose pastoral instructions were, however guardedly expressed, irreconcilable with any historic form of New England divinity.

Unlike the Great Awakening of 1740, the revival movement of the years from 1797 to 1801 was not attended by the outward physical manifestations which characterized that display of religious emotion. With very rare exceptions, and these chiefly among Baptist and Separatist assemblies, the bodily phenomena indicative of alarm or of hope, of joy or of distress, which then prevailed, were now absent. Compared with that revival, the manifestations of this one, like the presentations of truth with which they were associated, were distinctly, and even severely, intellectual.

Nor, unlike that former religious movement, did this one derive its impulse at all from the presence of a celebrated evangelist, or even from the use of the itineracy in any form. Some years were still to elapse, as we shall have occasion to note, before evangelistic itineracy was revived again. The work sprang up almost simultaneously throughout the churches under the ministrations of their own pastors, and progressed under the visible influence of only such added efforts and agencies as settled ministers are able mutually to afford one to another.

136 THE EVANGELICAL REAWAKENING.

A very considerable and exceedingly interesting body of revival narratives belonging to this period remains to us in the pages of the "Connecticut Evangelical Magazine," and in compilations derived from it, as well as in various pamphlets from the pens of many pastors of churches in different parts of New England where the work was conspicuously powerful. These narratives are, indeed, chiefly furnished by pastors sympathetic with New-Divinity views; and probably both the teachings they describe as having been most effectual in promoting the revival, and the experiences which they record of the converts made under it, may over-strongly emphasize the peculiarities of opinion in which they were differenced from their Old-Calvinist brethren. But we must avail ourselves of such resources as we have; and, after all, the revival was in an eminent degree a Hopkinsian one in its general character. So that we shall get close enough to its central and characterizing features by looking at it a moment through the eyes of some of those who, either as its promoters in the way of pastoral watch, or in the way of experience of its converting power, have left us record concerning it.

It is to be noticed that there was a great uniformity in the substance and proportion of doctrine enforced by the preachers. Rev. Alexander Gillet of Torrington, Connecticut, says:[1] —

"The doctrines made use of in carrying on this work, is another distinguishing feature of it. These are the

[1] *Connecticut Evangelical Magazine*, i. 135.

soul-humbling doctrines of our Saviour, which exalt God, and stain all the pride of human glory. The divine sovereignty — his universal government — the holiness, extent and inflexibility of the moral law — human depravity — our full dependence on God — the special agency of the Holy Spirit in conviction and conversion — and mere grace through Jesus Christ as the Mediator, and the only one: These have been kept constantly in view, more or less, and proved like a fire and hammer that breaketh the flinty rock in pieces."

Says Rev. Samuel Shepard of Lenox, Massachusetts, of his preaching:[1] —

These doctrines "are such as are usually termed *calvinistic*. Such truths, as the total and awful depravity of the human heart — the necessity of regeneration; . . . the equity of the divine law in its *penalty* as well as *precept* — the divine sovereignty in the salvation of sinners, as the only possible ground of hope in the case of a guilty offender — and all the doctrines essentially connected."

Rev. Increase Graves of Bridport, Vermont, writes:[2]—

"In our religious meetings, the doctrines insisted upon were the sovereignty of God, his purposes, total moral depravity, moral agency and accountableness, the circumstances which render human actions virtuous or vicious in the sight of God, justification solely by faith in Christ, the nature of saving faith and genuine

---

[1] *Connecticut Evangelical Magazine*, ii. 141.
[2] *New England Revivals*, Bennet Tyler (1846), p. 366.

repentance, the character of evangelical obedience, the obligations of men to do all they are able, just as much as if they could save themselves by their own works; the sure destruction of those who forbear all exertions, and of those also, who neglect to exert themselves in the right manner."

These quotations, taken almost at random from the reports of successful ministers in these different New England States, will indicate clearly enough the close, searching, dogmatic character of the pulpit inculcations of those times. And the most searching and alarming of these inculcations had a mysterious kind of acceptableness which the utterers of them attributed to the immediate energies of God's Spirit.

Rev. Jeremiah Hallock of Canton, Connecticut, records:[1] —

"What are called the hard sayings, such as the doctrines of total depravity, of the decrees, election, and the like, were popular."

And Rev. Ammi Robbins of Norfolk, Connecticut, says:[2] —

"Those doctrines which the world calls 'hard sayings' are the most powerful means in the hands of the blessed spirit, to pull down and destroy Satan's strong-holds in the hearts of sinners. No preaching, or conversation seems so effectual to drive them from their hiding places and refuges of lies, as to tell them plainly that

[1] Tyler's *Revivals*, p. 30.
[2] *Connecticut Evangelical Magazine*, i. 339.

they are eternally undone, if the unpromised mercy of God is not displayed in their favor; — that they have not the least claim on God, and if he does not have mercy they are gone forever; — that their eternal state is already fixed in the divine mind; and it concerns them to know what it is like to be; — that all they do short of real submission to God is wholly selfish; — that they may as well despair of ever helping themselves first as last; and that the reason why they don't find relief is merely because they will not yield and bow to a holy sovereign God."

To presentations of religious views so close-jointed and rigorous, it is not surprising that the response — as given in the experiences of those who in a time of intense spiritual awakening listened to and were molded by them — should have been equally marked and profound. Space will suffice for illustration on two or three points only.

The sense of sin, which has been seen in the course of these lectures to have been a prominent feature of religious experience at all periods of spiritual activity, was here; but here with a difference. It was here in a very powerful way, but as molded and defined by a particular philosophical explanation of the nature of sin; an explanation which, however involved in the teachings of Edwards as long before as the Great Awakening, had now become part of the common thought of the pulpit and the pews. Sin, in this view of it, was essentially selfishness; that is, preference of self to everything else, even to God; and so, in any point of contrast of interest and character between the divine and the human, really enmity to God.

We are, therefore, not surprised to find scores of such expressions of experience on this point as the following, taken almost haphazard, from the narratives of that time. One awakened inquirer comes to his pastor and says: [1] —

"I find that all I do is selfish. If I pray or read, it is all selfish."

Another, in the same condition, says: [2] —

"I see my heart so opposed to God, that I could not be happy were I admitted to heaven; and I should choose rather to be in hell than to dwell with God."

Still another is recorded as saying: [3] —

"I hated the Bible, because it contained my condemnation. I felt that God was partial in showing mercy to others and not to me. The enmity of my heart rose against him; and indeed, I wished there was no God. . . . I longed to be spoken out of existence, for the more I understood of the divine character, the more I hated it; and I could not endure the thought that the Lord reigned, and that all things were at his disposal. When I heard of some who had obtained comfort, and had not been so long in distress as I had, my heart boiled within me."

This sense of sin as opposition to God's laws, government, and character, and as even hatred to His

---

[1] Tyler's *Revivals*, p. 36.
[2] *Ibid.*, p. 27.
[3] *Ibid.*, p. 262.

THE SENSE OF SIN. 141

person, was a form of feeling which found very frequent expression. It is not at all an impeachment of its genuineness, or even of its accuracy of definition, however, to remind ourselves of its obvious connection with philosophical explanations of the nature of virtue which, to some extent certainly, gave to conceptions of sin a character that had not been recognized hitherto in any equivalent degree in the experiences of the religious life in New England.

Similarly characteristic of this new awakening, in comparison with any previous one, was the view inculcated and entertained in all New-Divinity circles respecting God's disregard of what were called " unregenerate doings." The language is archaic and uncouth, but the conception was anything but a scholastic one. It entered into the strenuous exhortations of the pulpit and the probing questionings of the room of anxious inquiry. God listens — it was affirmed by the most distinguished of divines — to no prayers of the unconverted. Dr. Samuel Hopkins wrote an elaborate treatise setting forth the alleged fact that the promises of the Gospel have no application whatever to unregenerate men.[1] All unregenerate praying is selfish, and therefore sin.

The thought was thrust into the turmoil of anxious souls under the darkest perturbations, with what has seemed to some its necessary addition of disquiet. From scores of recorded instances in the volumes referred to, take one only : [2] —

[1] *Enquiry Concerning the Promises of the Gospel*, Boston, 1768.
[2] Tyler's *Revivals*, p. 329.

"In July, when the attention to religion had become considerable, I began to find that I had not only a wicked heart, but that it was entirely selfish, and filled with the most dreadful and daring opposition to God; and that selfishness had been, and still was, the great moving impulse of all my actions.

"This put me to a great stand. . . . I now saw that the prayers of the wicked are an abomination unto the Lord. Yet I was told that prayer was a duty incumbent upon me notwithstanding my own sinfulness, and that I ought to pray with a penitent heart. This was what I could not bear, and I found myself actually at war with God Almighty."

But the experience of converts answered to the demand; as, indeed, is usual in similar cases. Their "conviction of their selfish regards in all their attempts to pray led them to reflect that *their prayer was sin.*"[1] Their persuasion of the sinfulness of all "unregenerate doings" created in them a "uniformity of sentiment" that a "change of heart . . . is in answer to no prayer made by the subject before it takes place."[2]

These processes and convictions of mind seem to have been very general. They led easily on to another widely characterizing feature of this great religious awakening — the inculcation and exercise of the duty of "unconditional submission" to God's will, even to the extent of readiness to be lost, if the highest interests of the universe demand it.

[1] *Evangelical Magazine*, i. 463.
[2] Tyler's *Revivals*, p. 369.

There has been occasion to see that, at earlier periods of the religious history of the New England churches, substantially the same conception of duty was entertained. Hooker and Shepherd inculcated it at the very opening of American Gospel teachings.[1] Mrs. Edwards felt, and her husband practically advocated, this conception of Christian experience in the Awakening of 1740–1742.

Dr. Emmons, himself an inculcator of this duty of unconditional submission, does, however, attempt to distinguish between the idea as Shepherd and Hooker taught it, and as New-Divinity teachers presented it. He says:[2] —

"I know indeed that Mr. Hooker and Mr. Shepherd maintained, that a sinner under awakening and conviction must be willing to be cast off forever, in order to prepare him for regeneration or true conversion. This we acknowledge is an erroneous opinion; and no Hopkinsian that I am acquainted with, adopts this opinion."

But the distinction between Emmons's view and Hooker's is more scholastic than practical. Emmons says that Hooker demanded this experience before conversion, as one of the preliminary steps to prepare for conversion. Emmons assigns it a place in conversion as one of the accompaniments of the regenerative change. One can but think that if these two men could have talked together half an hour, they would have seen that they meant the same thing.

[1] *Ante*, p. 28.
[2] Letter on Moses Stuart's Sermon, Park's *Emmons*, p. 398.

144 THE EVANGELICAL REAWAKENING.

The argument by which this duty of unconditional submission even to be cast off forever, if need be, was enforced, is clearly put by an early missionary of the American Board, Rev. Gordon Hall:[1] —

"The benevolent mind must consent to the misery of a part, that the whole may be perfect. This suffering part must be fixed, bearing a certain proportion to the whole. It must likewise be composed of a definite number of individuals. To this the benevolent mind must consent. Now if the benevolent mind sees, that this suffering part cannot be secured to its exact proportion without its including himself, must he not acquiesce? And if he is unwilling to be included in this part, does he not place himself in opposition to the perfection of the system? The truth in this case, I think, cannot be mistaken."

As this duty of submission was presented in the revival of the last years of the eighteenth century, it obviously took a powerful hold, not merely on the processes of men's intellects, but on the operations of their wills and hearts in the crisis-hours of their spiritual experience. To quote a few examples: Rev. Dr. Griffin, writing of the condition of things in New Hartford, Connecticut, in 1798 and 1799, says:[2] —

"The subjects of it [the revival] have generally expressed a choice that God should pursue the 'determinate counsel' of his own will, and without consulting

---

[1] Park's *Emmons*, p. 189.
[2] *Evangelical Magazine*, i. 221.

them, decide respecting their salvation. To the question whether they expected to alter the divine mind by prayer, it has been answered, 'I sometimes think, if this were possible I should not dare to pray.' . . . Many have expressed a willingness to put their names to a blank, and leave it with God to fill it up; and *that*, because his having the government would secure the termination of all things in his own glory."

Another pastor, Rev. Samuel J. Mills of Torringford, Connecticut, father of the more famous Samuel, records [1] as the characteristic attitude of the converts of the revival coming under his observation, that: —

"They have been brought to resign themselves cheerfully, without any reserve, into the hands of God, to be disposed of as may be most for his glory — rejoicing that they were, and might be, in the hands of such an holy, just and wise God, let their future situation be what it might."

Still another, Rev. Jeremiah Hallock of Canton, Connecticut, gives as the language of an inquirer in his congregation, and as language typical of the feelings of inquirers generally: [2] —

"I wish you would pray for me that I may be converted, if God can convert me, consistently with his pleasure and glory. If not, I do not desire it. I wish also you would pray for my poor children, that God would convert them; not that they are any better, or their souls worth any more than my neighbors'."

---

[1] *Evangelical Magazine*, i. pp. 28, 29.
[2] Tyler's *Revivals*, p. 32.

Such, in a large and general way, were the characteristics of a religious awakening which, far more profoundly than that of 1740, took hold on the real life of New England piety, and which brought into the churches a great body of members — it is difficult to estimate how many — bearing a stamp of experience so deep, and on the whole so genuine, that they were of inestimable value to every interest of the Christian kingdom.

But this awakening, of the last three or four years preceding the opening of the present century, is with difficulty regarded as an event by itself. It was rather the beginning of a series of such events, repeated at irregular intervals for many subsequent years. In 1805 and 1806, there were great religious quickenings in many towns in Massachusetts and Rhode Island. Again, from 1815 to 1818, a wave of spiritual impulse passed over the churches, reaching especially with its blessings those of Vermont and New Hampshire. The years 1820–1823, and 1826–1828, were again years of great spiritual refreshing; and yet more powerfully those of 1830–1831, and 1840–1845; while what as yet appears to be the last of this series or group of revivalistic manifestations on any extensive geographical scale — and itself somewhat distinctly differenced in character from its predecessors — occurred as late as 1857–1859.

These spiritual stirrings, reaching over a period of sixty years, are properly enough grouped together as possessing a general similarity of character. But

EVANGELISTIC METHODS. 147

there was, in the first few years following 1797, the year which marked their commencement, a gradual modification either of their outward method, or of the balance and proportion of doctrinal statement by which they were promoted, which a careful observer of the religious life developed by them cannot wholly overlook. It was remarked that, at first, few or no itinerating agencies were employed. When assistance was required, as, in the stress of multiplied preaching services and inquiry meetings it was naturally often needed, the services of eminent pastors who had been signally successful in their own fields, like Nathan Strong, Edward Dorr Griffin, Jeremiah Hallock and Timothy M. Cooley, were made use of to aid and reinforce the efforts of the home laborer. But, as time went on, and as recurrent occasions of awakened interest laid their heavy burdens on pastoral endeavor, evangelistic labor was called in to supplement, and in some cases to direct, in the conduct of revival seasons.

Rev. Asahel Nettleton, one of the earliest and most successful of these itinerating evangelists, was soon followed by Rev. Charles G. Finney, and they by a very considerable succession of more or less able and useful laborers, among whom may be mentioned Rev. Messrs. E. N. Kirk, Jacob Knapp, and Jedediah Burchard. But, as there was occasion to notice in connection with the evangelistic features of the Great Awakening of 1740–1742, so here, evangelism had its drawbacks. A very considerable number of ill-equipped and indiscreet exhorters felt constrained to enter the field as revivalists, introducing measures of more than questionable expediency, often alienating pastors and people, and, in some instances, dividing churches through the results of their extravagant and unwise procedures.

Methods, too, unknown to the earlier period of the awakening, came into more or less accepted employment, like the "four-days' meetings," and the "anxious seat," as it was called. Dr. Emmons, himself a strenuous Hopkinsian and an earnest revivalist, opposed from the outset these "four-days' meetings," as tending to fix attention on the form of promoting an awakening rather than on the power by which the awakening was itself energized. Ultimately, probably, his objections were justified, the "four-days' meetings" becoming a kind of religious fetish; but, for a while, they, and even the "anxious seat," — to which, as employed by Mr. Finney, both Mr. Nettleton and Dr. Beecher strongly demurred,[1] — seemed to be useful instruments in carrying on the revival work.

More important, though less a matter of observation, as period succeeded to period in this more than a half-century of successive waves of religious quickening, were certain intellectual and doctrinal changes — which were partially recognizable at the time, but are now more clearly discerned — in the preaching which accompanied these awakenings. Not, indeed, that these changes were uniform and

[1] Letters of the Rev. Dr. Beecher and Rev. Mr. Nettleton on the *New Measures in promoting Revivals of Religion* [1828].

universal. On the contrary, the extreme Hopkinsian type of doctrine, which was so general in 1797, was never without its occasional exponents in any awakening afterward. It found, indeed, as to some of its main positions, one of its ablest advocates in Rev. Charles G. Finney during the revival of 1857–1859, at Boston. While conducting a series of meetings in Park Street Church at this period, Mr. Finney, in a sermon from the text in Proverbs, "The plowing of the wicked is sin," set forth a view of the guiltiness and the obnoxiousness to God of all actions of men antecedent to conversion, the strenuousness of which no Hopkinsian or Emmonsite could ever have surpassed.

But, after all, a certain real, however often insensible, change was gradually altering the tone and emphasis of the revival utterances. There was a shading away of the Hopkinsian peculiarities. There was less insistence on the utter inutility of all endeavors of men to bring themselves into a way of repentance and faith; and there was less demand for the particular form of self-renunciation which had been called — perhaps inexactly but popularly — a "willingness to be damned." As a consequence, the type of experience developed in connection with the awakenings of 1830–1831 and 1840–1841 shows a clear variation from that of earlier revivals; while, respecting the awakening of 1857–1859, there was so marked a change, especially in the absence of any considerable doctrinal impress or of any profound sense of sin, that some good men who remembered former awakenings were almost disposed to question its genuineness.

Two causes combined to effect this progressive alteration in the type of revival utterances.

One was the position taken, on the question of "unregenerate doings," by a man who by all antecedents of birth and education — as Edwards's grandson and Yale College's graduate and president — ought to have been a docile follower of the Newport divine. On the contrary, President Dwight sided on this point with Old-Calvinists like Phillips and Hemmenway and Hart, and taught[1] that "Ministers ought to advise and exhort sinners to use the Means of Grace." He affirmed, indeed, that all actions previous to regeneration, so far as they possess a moral quality, are sinful; but that in the "cries of a suffering creature for mercy" he was unable to hear anything "of a sinful nature," or to see any reason why "the prayers of such a sinner may not be objects of Divine Benevolence." And, in general, as to the performance or non-performance of so-called religious actions by unregenerate men, he argued that both in respect to society, the man himself, and the quality of the action in its own nature, the man was "less sinful when he performs the act than when he neglects or refuses to perform it." This moderate and practical view of the nature of "unregenerate doings" was essentially that which Old-Calvinism had maintained. The controversy between Hopkins

[1] *Theology* iv. pp. 38–74.

and West on the one side, and Hart, Hemmenway, and Moses Mather on the other, had been long continued and voluminous on this point. But the Old-Calvinist position was now adopted by a man who by blood and breeding should have been a Hopkinsian; a man, moreover, who spoke with the persuasiveness of an eloquent orator from that position of conspicuity and influence, the college pulpit. Dwight's plain, luminous manner of discourse, leveled to the easy apprehension of average men and of college students, did much to modify, as the revival era went on, the extremer statements which accompanied its opening.

The other source of an altered tone, discernible in the later stages of the revivalistic epoch, was the appeal made to self-love as a legitimate motive to repentance and a change of heart by what came to be known as "New Haven Theology," as developed by Rev. Nathaniel W. Taylor. Here, again, it may be said that the New Haven Divinity did little more, on this point, than revert to the Old-Calvinist position. The question of the possibility of a sinless, and even of a virtuous and beneficent, self-love had been a distinct and elaborately argued matter of debate between Hopkins and Hemmenway, Mather and Hart, to the extent of many an acrimonious and toilsome pamphlet half a century before.

Dr. Taylor and his followers did, indeed, assert that true self-love and disinterested benevolence were not variant, but harmonious. But to Hopkinsians, who identified self-love with sinfulness, and whose whole phraseology of argument and exhortation was framed to that conception, the idea was obnoxious that there was any sense in which regard to himself by an unregenerate man could be the ground of legitimate evangelical appeal. Very likely the phrase "self-love" was, in the existing state of New England theological dialect, an unfortunate one to express the idea of that regard to one's full and highest interests which Dr. Taylor meant to signify by it. But Bishop Butler had used the phrase, and in the same significance, a hundred years before. The Hopkinsian vocabulary had, however, no room for the term except for uses of denunciation.

So far as the view of the New Haven school prevailed, it necessarily modified the Hopkinsian position, to which it was opposed; and it certainly did modify the extremer forms of Hopkinsian expression even in the case of many preachers who did not accept the New Haven Theology. So that the later awakenings of 1830-1831, 1840-1841, and 1857-1859 were, in the preaching which attended them and in the experiences developed by them, much less distinctively marked by the Hopkinsian type than were those earlier in the series.

Taken as a whole, however, it cannot well be questioned that the movement derived its main source and received its chief impulse from that school of New England thought which — from the uncompromising vigor with which Samuel Hopkins set forth the main principles of its close-jointed and robust theology — has come to bear the name of that solemn thinker of Great Barrington and Newport.

The importance of this general revival movement, reaching as it did over two generations of New England life, cannot possibly be overestimated. Whether sympathized with or disliked, its significance as a great mental and-moral phenomenon was never approached in magnitude by any other religious movement in New England. For, aside from those effects on the individual and collective religious life of the people who came under its power that constitute the results of the revival with which these lectures have primarily to do, there were other more organic and institutional effects too closely related to the awakening to allow them to be passed by wholly unnoticed.

The great missionary movements, home and foreign alike, in the Congregational and Baptist denominations, which characterized the early years of this century, had their roots in the revival.

The General Association of Connecticut, in the year 1798, resolved itself into the Connecticut Missionary Society, with the avowed purpose " to Christianize the Heathen in North America and to support and promote Christian knowledge in the New Settlements of the United States." To promote this enterprise, it began to publish the " Connecticut Evangelical Magazine " in 1800, and received its charter of incorporation in 1802. Following Connecticut, only a year later, Massachusetts formed its Missionary Society in 1799, and in 1803 established its "Missionary Magazine" for the purpose of promoting intelligence on the subject. New Hampshire established a similar Society in 1801, and Vermont in 1807.

The Baptists were hardly behindhand — handicapped though they had been by adverse legislation and social disadvantage — in this newly awakened zeal for the extension of the Gospel. In Massachusetts they organized a Missionary Society in 1802, and in the following year began the publication of a magazine in its interest. Connecticut Baptists came into missionary organization in 1811.

The societies thus far mentioned — to which a Religious Tract Society in Vermont in 1808, and Bible Societies in Massachusetts and Connecticut in 1809, might appropriately be added — were all organized for evangelistic work in our own land. But the newly kindled sense of responsibility for the souls of other men — a view of duty which was the natural and necessary result of the New-Divinity doctrine of benevolence — could not content itself with endeavors after the lost in America only. Was not the whole world lying in wickedness? Had it not been the fond anticipation of Jonathan Edwards, nearly seventy years before, when he wrote his treatise designed to "promote a Visible Union of God's People in Extraordinary Prayer for the Revival of Religion and the Advancement of Christ's Kingdom on Earth," that the time for the

Gospel's proclamation to all nations had nearly come? Had not grim Samuel Hopkins, as long ago as 1773, united with Dr. Ezra Stiles in an appeal to the churches to send missionaries to Africa, as well as to liberate African bondmen held in American slavery? Missionary endeavor could no longer limit itself to American soil; and so the year 1810 saw the organization of the American Board of Commissioners for Foreign Missions, designed for the joint coöperation of Congregationalists and Presbyterians in carrying the Gospel to heathen shores. Baptist Christians in Massachusetts followed, two years later, with the "Salem Bible Translation and Foreign Missionary Society," which was the forerunner of their Missionary Union, organized in 1814; and the Methodist Missionary Society came into being in 1819.

In a very similar way, the parentage of Andover, Bangor, New Haven, and East Windsor — now Hartford — Theological Seminaries among the Congregationalists, and Newton Theological Institution among the Baptists, is distinctly traceable to the revival influences of the opening part of the century. The seminary at Andover, founded in 1808, was the result of a joint movement of an Old-Calvinist party and of a Hopkinsian one, on the basis of a creed, drawn up with almost incredible painstaking, to include just as much of the peculiarities of each party as would not exclude the participation in the resultant symbol of the other; — a creed which was established as the standard of doctrine "permanent"... "as the moon and stars forever."

The seminary at East Windsor, founded in 1834, was planted to offset the errors into which its supporters believed the New Haven institution had fallen, through the leadership of Dr. Taylor and his conceptions of sin and the office of self-love; at the latter of which alleged errors we had occasion to glance a few moments ago. But, differing in what may be called their secondary cause as these various institutions did, and expressive as they were of at least four recognizably diverse tendencies or habitudes of thought on certain speculative points of theology in New England, they all, and all equally, came out of the heat and glow of the revival movement of the century's opening days; were primarily identical in their purpose to uphold, and to qualify their students to uphold, that Gospel the fundamentals of which they all held; and in their very variousness were a witness, not to the meagerness, but to the abounding vigor and fullness, of New England's religious life.

Nor would it be right wholly to overlook, among the less organic, but perhaps not less important, results of the two generations of revival movements, certain considerable changes wrought in other directions having a distinct bearing on the type of religious life in New England.

The opening of the revival era, in 1797, saw the Half-way-Covenant system, though sorely wounded and argumentatively discredited, still largely in operation among the churches. Before the close of the period it had vanished from existence. The

SOCIAL USAGES MODIFIED. 157

system could not stand the intense emphasis which the series of awakenings had put upon the necessity of personal religious experience as the only proper condition of membership in a Christian church. And so, long before this series of awakenings had terminated, the system, founded on another and incompatible theory of church-fellowship, itself died. Gradually waning, apparently its last breath was drawn about 1825 or 1828.

An interesting and important change, too, came about in this period, which largely modified the general habits of the Christian community in reference to temperance and to certain forms of social amusement. At the opening of the era under present review, ardent spirits were in quite general use among religious people; were furnished at most social and ecclesiastical gatherings; were tendered by ministers of the Gospel to their calling brethren and to parishional visitors; while a not infrequent accompaniment of the induction of a new minister into his office was a dinner well set out with alcoholic inspirations, followed in the evening by an ordination ball.

So distinguished and able a minister as Rev. Nathan Strong of the First Church, Hartford, Connecticut, was not discredited in character by owning and conducting a distillery plant within sixty rods of his church door. From 1790 to 1796 — the year before the great revivals commenced — the business was an extensive one on the pastor's part. The records of Hartford land transfers show some twenty deeds of real estate, involving thirty or forty thousand dollars' worth of property, bought and sold by Mr. Strong and his brother-in-law, Reuben Smith, under the title of Reuben Smith & Co., the pastor's name generally taking the priority in the deeds made to or by the partners. Other transactions related to the vats, stills, and cooper shops used in the prosecution of their enterprise.

The close of the period under survey saw the general banishment of wines and liquors, alike from convivial household use and from special festive occasions. Exceptions doubtless existed, but they were exceptions soberly animadverted upon and only the more confirmative of the rule. While, not only was the ordination ball discontinued, but balls in general were, in all evangelical circles, discountenanced; and even private, social dancing was generally frowned upon as incompatible with that severer standard of morals and religion which the revival had begotten.

Meantime, to turn our attention for a moment to the so-called Liberal School in religious matters referred to at the outset of this lecture, — and in so doing to bring our survey to a close, — it is to be said that there was change and progress here as well as among theologians of the older types.

The representatives of Liberal Theology were not numerous, and they were limited in locality almost entirely to eastern Massachusetts. But they were cultivated and able men. They occupied many of the leading pulpits of Boston and its vicinity, and they challenged a well-nigh controlling influence in the government of Harvard College. The very different conception they had come to entertain of the sinfulness of man's nature, and of the necessity of the direct interposing energies of the Divine Spirit for man's rescue, had long made a great contrast between the tone of their inculcations and those of either the Old-Calvinists or the Hopkinsians about them. The character of their preaching is well illustrated in the peroration of the sermon of Rev. William Emerson, father of Ralph Waldo Emerson, and pastor of the First Church in Boston, which was delivered some years before anything like a formal separation of the Boston churches into Orthodox and Unitarian had come to pass, on the interesting occasion of the entrance of that old church of Cotton, Norton, Davenport, Allen, and Foxcroft into a new house of worship. The genial and accomplished pastor of this historic organization, pointing out the value of the sanctuary of divine worship as preparing for the rest of the heavenly home, concludes with this appeal:[1] —

"Let us be virtuous, my brethren, and this presence of God, this rest, shall be ours. By a proper reverence of God's house and worship on earth, we shall obtain a seat in the mansions of heaven."

But more vigorous advocates of what it was the custom of the time to call a "rational theology"

[1] *Historical Sketch of the First Church in Boston* [1812], p. 256.

were in the field than the kindly pastor of the Boston First Church.

William Ellery Channing had been installed at the Federal Street Church in June, 1803. In November, 1803, the "Monthly Anthology" began to be published as an organ of liberal thought and as an offset to the teachings of the Orthodox "Massachusetts Missionary Magazine." Joseph Stevens Buckminster became pastor at the Brattle Street Church in January, 1805. In February of this same year, the struggle for the chair of the Hollis Professorship of Divinity in Harvard College, which had been made vacant by the death of the Old-Calvinist, Dr. David Tappan, terminated, after two years of contest, in the appointment of Rev. Henry Ware, the Liberal candidate, — an event which marked the transference of this first-born child of Puritanism, and school of its prophets for nearly six generations, from the Orthodox to the Liberal side. Events now moved forward with more celerity. The alarm felt at what was regarded as a subversion of the original intent of the fathers in the foundation of Harvard College, drove the Orthodox, both of the Old-Calvinist and the Hopkinsian schools, to unite in the establishment of a new theological seminary at Andover, opened, as has been said, in 1808. The impulse of this event, followed, in 1809, by the organization of Park Street Church in Boston on a definitely outspoken evangelical creed, and the coming into the adjacent ministry of three able exponents of Orthodox views — Joshua Huntington at the Old South

Church, Boston, in 1808, John Codman at Dorchester in the same year, and Edward Dorr Griffin at the newly formed Park Street Church, in 1811 — gave to the evangelical party a stimulus which had long been lacking in the somewhat rarefied atmosphere of Boston liberalism. The lines were thus, month by month, more definitely drawn. "The Monthly Anthology" on the one side, and the "Panoplist," which had been established as the evangelical organ in 1805, on the other, kept the issues in debate before the popular eye. The annual sermons before the Massachusetts Ministerial Conventions were made the occasion of more formal presentations of the same issues to the clerical mind. In his sermon on such an occasion in 1810, Rev. Dr. Porter of Roxbury said, concerning the doctrines of : —

"Original Sin, a Trinity in Unity, the Mere Humanity, Super-Angelic Nature, or Absolute Deity of Christ, and the Absolute Eternity of Punishment . . . I cannot place my finger on any one article in the list of doctrines just mentioned, the belief or rejection of which I consider essential to the Christian faith or character."

To such a statement as this, on an occasion so public and official, it is not surprising that the adherents of the older faith should respond by declining any longer to afford to those whose views it represented that sign of fellowship in doctrine implied in pulpit exchange, — a course of action which, originated by Dr. Codman of Dorchester, and sustained by ecclesiastical councils, did much to make visible to the general eye a line of cleavage which had long existed in spirit.

An almost fortuitously raised discussion in 1815, over a chapter on "American Unitarianism" in an English book — Belsham's "Life of Lindsey" — widened the breach, and as a recent Unitarian historian of his own denomination has said,[1] availed to "force the hand" of the Liberals and to compel their adoption of a cognomen which they had not been quite ready to accept.

But the cleavage was now really complete. "Rational Theology," as its advocates preferred to call it, had become a distinct, though geographically circumscribed, factor in New England religious thought.

Whatever was still lacking in its doctrinal indication of separation was supplied by the sermon of Channing at the ordination of Rev. Jared Sparks at Baltimore in 1819; and the celebrated Dedham decision of the Massachusetts Supreme Court in 1820, the ultimate effect of which was to give above eighty societies, historically connected with Orthodox churches, into Unitarian control, sufficiently marks the status of the new party on the ecclesiastical side. Henceforth, for good or ill, Liberalism — ranging in degree from the Arianism of Channing to the Rationalism of Parker — was a factor to be taken account of in all estimates of New England's religious life. It was on the soil first settled by the Puritans that this altered view, alike of God and of

---

[1] Allen's *Unitarianism since the Reformation*, p. 192.

man, had its American beginnings, and in the pulpits of the successors of Elder Brewster, John Cotton, and Increase Mather that it became most strongly intrenched. So largely did it dominate Boston and its immediate vicinity that Dr. Lyman Beecher, writing of the time of his arrival in that city in 1823, said, with some little exaggeration perhaps, but with substantial truth: —

"All the literary men of Massachusetts were Unitarian; all the trustees and professors of Harvard College were Unitarian; all the *élite* of wealth and fashion crowded Unitarian churches; the judges on the bench were Unitarian, giving decisions by which the peculiar features of church organization so carefully ordered by the Pilgrim Fathers had been nullified."

Over against Old-Calvinism and New-Divinity alike, or any modification of them which holds to the sinfulness and loss of human nature, the necessity and reality of a divine atonement, and redemption by interposing grace, there were now found, — what apparently are long to continue as disagreeing and opposing currents in the religious life of our New England churches and communities, — the conceptions of human nature as dignified and undepraved, of salvation by cultivation rather than by faith, of self-acquired character as the ground of divine acceptance and of the intellectual and moral unity of God and man.

It is not the design of these lectures to pronounce between positions so opposite and irreconcilable.

V.

THE CURRENT PERIOD.

In approaching the aspect of the religious life of New England to be considered in this lecture some embarrassment necessarily arises. It is the embarrassment which always attends an attempt to state impartially the true character and significance of current traits and tendencies. If, even when things are set in a background of historic perspective, it is very difficult to present them with perfect justice to the eye, much more is it so when he who speaks and they who hear are in a manner a part of the things spoken of; when they have been molded by the influences which have made the period what it is; are in the very current of its flow, and have, almost inevitably, a definite feeling of satisfaction or of disquiet respecting the condition of things about them, and the direction in which they are seemingly making progress. The embarrassment cannot be avoided, however, except at the cost of not attempting to make, or at least not attempting to express, any estimate respecting what after all is the most interesting period to every man, — his own period, — and of having no opinion whatever concerning that which concerns him most.

THE CIVIL WAR.   165

Doing, then, the best possible, let as impartial a survey as circumstances permit be taken of the aspect of the religious life presented in New England in that portion of its history which, for convenience, may be considered as reaching from the last event spoken of in the previous lecture — the revival of 1857-1859 — to the present time, — a period, that is, of about thirty-seven years.

The epoch opened in the thick of the great political and moral debate on the slavery question in the United States, — a debate which was just about passing from the arena of discussion with tongue and pen to the field of arms and blood.

All the country over, but especially here in New England, the moral sense of the people had been for years in a process of strenuous exercise and education in reference to the great public wrong and danger of the chattel bondage of men and women, multitudes of whom were as truly and as formally members of the Church of Christ in this land as were any of its inhabitants. The crime against man and the sin against God, of this great iniquity, had slowly indeed, but surely and at last irresistibly, been coming home to men's bosoms, till what was stigmatized on the floor of Congress as the "New England conscience," which was in truth pretty much also the whole Northern conscience, became thoroughly aroused. What followed is written in letters of fire and blood on the ineffaceable pages of history.

The war was a great patriotic outburst of emotion

and energy, the central and vivifying principle of which was a moral one. For the time, all lesser or baser interests were in most minds subordinated to the great and dominating claims of patriotism and humanity.

It is not strange, that under the pressure of this outgoing and absorbing interest in public and racial concerns, the more private considerations of individual relationship to religious truth and to the Christian Church should have been relatively obscured. That would be but natural, — nay, inevitable.

But, however prepared for that result, the consequences of the great moral upheaval were somewhat disappointing, nevertheless. Some observers, arrived at years of reflection and forecast at the time, anticipated from the impulse and inspiration of the generous and heroic sentiments of the hour, and especially from the moral elements of sacrifice and beneficence associated with them, an altogether permanent and decided uplift of the religious life of the people to a higher level, — a distinct spiritualizing and purifying of the conditions of society, which would make the power of piety in individual hearts more controlling, and the progress of all true interests of the Church of Christ and the Kingdom of God more rapid and certain.

It is needless to say that while some of these anticipations have in part been realized, not all of them have been. Hardly more necessary is it to say why they have not been.

War, anyway, and for an object however high or important, is attended and followed by its inevitable demoralizations. Not a war of human history but has been so accompanied or succeeded. From the day when the Master in the Garden said to his impetuous disciple, Peter, eager to serve his cause, — "Put up thy sword again into his place; for all they that take the sword shall perish with the sword," — to this day, war has been a poor promoter of religion. Although it may possibly be true, as Hosea Biglow has it, that —

> ". . . . civlyzation doos git forrid
> Sometimes upon a powder-cart," —

the Gospel of Christ does not advance much in that way.

But, laying aside the question of the general influence of war upon the moral and spiritual life of a people, and the influence of our war upon our people in particular, there were certain accompaniments and sequences of the conflict which especially tended to frustrate that high expectation which some entertained of a visible, certain, and permanent moral and spiritual uplift of the public life to higher levels.

One such frustrative influence was the introduction at that era into the general spirit of the people of an eagerness for sudden and splendid success — in accumulation of property, in achievement of social or political distinction — such as had never in any even approximate degree characterized our communities before. Amid all the sufferings and self-denials of the many, the few grew rich or famous or variously successful with a celerity and an apparent ease that has been like an intoxicant to society ever since. A hunger and restlessness for rapid achievement and prosperity entered then into the people's blood, whose fever still shows no signs of dying out; and whose manifested tokens are one of the most ominous signs of our times to-day.

When, to the simplicity of Puritan beginnings, and to the sober frugality of even the middle period of our national history, there has succeeded in wide circles of society a prodigality and a luxury which Rome scarcely in her splendors could surpass, the problem becomes a grave one alike for morals and for religion: — what is, and is to be, the issue of these things? This is mainly a *post-bellum* phenomenon. The great fortunes of the day — the wonder of the world and the provocation of envy and anarchy — are, with few exceptions, the product of the brief years which lie between us and the surrender at Appomattox; but they stand more closely related to the ambitions and acquisitions begotten in the period of the rebellion than is always remembered.

Nor has it been without a very considerable abatement of the expectation of a high moral elevation of sentiment which should forever after characterize our social and public life, that we find the Nation called upon, ten, twenty, and thirty years

SPIRITUAL RESULTS OF THE WAR. 169

after the war, to support a pension-list — now costing more than the standing army of any nation of Europe, — for services which were supposed to be the spontaneous and irrepressible offering of patriotic and humanitarian sentiment; and that we see both the great political parties of the country using this pension list as the reckless means of outbidding one another in popular favor.

On the other hand, it is cheerfully to be recognized that the war gave an impulse, immense and lasting, to arts, inventions, industries, mechanisms, commercial and manufacturing enterprises, certainly not evil in themselves, and many of them distinctly tributary to social and public welfare. If any, or even many, of them have indirectly worked to the disadvantage of moral and religious interests, it is only because anything in this world of ours may be made inimical to those interests by too engrossing attention, turning away men's minds and hearts from other less visible realities.

But, however it may be viewed, the great cyclonic event which marked the beginning of the epoch whose religious traits are occupying present attention, constitutes a reckoning point and a divisional boundary in American history. Things on one or the other side of that separating mountain-barrier are manifoldly diverse. In politics, in business, in society, and, as there will be occasion also to see, in religion as well, things are in many respects in a different era. It is not the purpose of this lecture to say whether, or in what respects, the era is better or worse than any before, but only to report as clearly as possible some of its distinguishing characteristics.

One feature of current religious life in New England, so obvious and familiar as to call for no extended remark, — only for passing mention, indeed, — is the immense development of the principle of voluntary organization for moral and religious objects characteristic of the present time. There was occasion to notice in a previous lecture the somewhat sudden emergence, near the beginning of the present century, and under the impulse of the evangelistic spirit then prevailing in the churches, of quite a number of such voluntary organizations for missionary and educational purposes in several ecclesiastical denominations. Yet the development of the principle then illustrated was but infantile when compared with that which has marked the history of the past thirty-five years. Into the statistics of this matter it is impossible here even to begin to look; but it is only needful to bring to mind the names of such organizations as the Young Men's and Young Women's Christian Associations, the Christian Endeavor Society, the Brotherhood of Philip and Andrew, the Epworth League, the Salvation Army, the King's Daughters, and many others for religious purposes; the Red Cross Society, the Shelters, Bands of Mercy, and Social Settlements, the Woman's Christian Temperance Union, and the various industrial relief societies for humanitarian and philanthropic ends; the Chautauqua Circles, Summer Schools, and University Extension classes for instructional purposes, — to have presented to us an amount and a variety of organization for educational, moral, and religious aims of which nothing in past history affords anything more than a suggestion. A very few of these corporate and wide-extended forms of benevolent or religious endeavor had their origin or introduction on the other side of that boundary line which has been spoken of as dividing the current period of New England's religious life from the past; but most of them were born this side of that boundary, and all of them have had their chief illustration distinctly this side of it, and within the lives of those who are still young men and women.

Ramifications of nearly all of these organizations reach to almost every farmhouse threshold and factory door; and these, supplemented by multitudinous lesser local associations for kindred purposes, and aided by the ever-increasing volume of the publications of the religious and philanthropic press, afford at once an indication of and a channel for a form of benevolent or of religious activity wholly characteristic of very recent days in amount and facility for expression.

This being the case, it is not surprising that another prevailing feature of current religious life, when compared with the past, is what, without any invidiousness in the designation, may be called its outwardness of character. Almost everything about the religious life of the present hour tends to the external rather than to the internal. The means ready to every Christian's hand for active employment, and the manifold objects of effort, more or less distinctively religious, clamorously soliciting their use, call almost every willing worker forth from himself, and the consideration of his personal interests, into the alacrities of speech or deed for other men. What the grandparents of the generation now on the stage of action used to consider a main duty of the spiritual life — the duty of self-examination — has little, or indeed almost no, place in modern experience. The habit, once so general, of solemn, privately recorded covenants on conscious entrance into the religious life, and of frequently subsequent review of fidelity to such self-imposed engagements, may be said to have gone by altogether. If it now exists at all, it is, and is regarded as being, the idiosyncrasy of special conscientiousness almost bordering on morbidness, rather than as the natural expression of healthy religious feeling.

The quietudes of old-time meditation and the scrutiny of aims and motives are departed. They relate to a lost art; nor is it easy to see how, under present conditions of life, the art can be found again, if it were desirable to be found. The watchwords of a not very remote religious past were "consider," "be," "become;" those of the present are "resolve," "speak," "do." We have not, probably, the results sufficiently in hand fully to determine the significance and the remoter consequences of this change, but it is plain that it involves a very distinct modification of the general type of the religious life, when compared with that which existed on the other side of our boundary of thirty-five or forty years ago.

Closely connected with what has just been spoken of, but itself constituting a distinct feature of current religious life, is the changed conception of the experiences properly qualificative for membership in the Christian Church. It is needless to bring again to mind the very definite and profound character of those intellectual and emotional exercises of the spirit, once so general, and once regarded as so indispensable. It was remarked, in the last lecture, that even so far back as the revival period of 1857–1859, grave questionings were entertained by many observers of previous religious awakenings as to the genuineness and lastingness of that one, owing to the contrast it afforded in the comparatively slight intensity of the experiences of its subjects, when measured by what had been customary in earlier New England history. This lessened intensity was noticeable in various particulars, but was especially observable respecting the matter of consciousness of sin. Here it was very plain that a marked difference existed. The sense of sin, so vivid a feature of experience in all revival periods hitherto, was singularly vague and unemphatic.

But if this was true in that last of the large, pervasive religious awakenings of American history, much more so has it been in the years which have succeeded. As a general fact of current religious experience for the generation now on the stage, the Christian profession and entrance into the membership of the Church have been attended by no considerable struggles of spirit; by no very humiliating feelings of guilt and desert of condemnation; by no profound and over-mastering realization that salvation, if received, is a matter of unmerited grace alone; nor even by any very considerable changes in conscious tastes or purposes in life. The observation is too widespread and too uniform to permit of doubt on this matter, that, to whatsoever cause it may be ascribed, an alteration not only of a very distinct, but of a very deep, nature has characterized the recent type of religious experience in these matters. Children and youth presenting themselves for what — by way of deference to historic usage apparently — is still called "examination" for church-membership, students of theology offering themselves for licensure to preach the Gospel, and candidates for ordination before church councils, all illustrate, and illustrate almost equally, the change spoken of. It is no exaggeration to say that, though the Congregational churches of New England and of the country at large have rejected the Half-way-Covenant theory, they are to-day generally admitting to full communion a membership which exhibits less clearly understood and realized convictions of sin and of the necessity of atoning grace as the only hope of lost men than under that system were often expected of those who came only halfway within the covenant doors. A distinct practical approximation is thus indicated to that Episcopal theory of the Church as a mixed body, among whose various elements it is impossible to discriminate in this world, — a theory which it was the primary object of original Congregationalism to repudiate and escape from. For it cannot be gravely pretended that the conditions now generally pre-requisite to church-membership are such as meet that demand of "visible saintship" on which ancient Congregationalism would alone build its churchly edifice. The modern practice may be an improvement on the old theory, but it is scarcely possible not to recognize the change. Congregationalism to-day, in reference to this matter, is being worked on Episcopalian principles; and it is being so worked with decidedly less adequate safeguards against mistake and lack of preparation for intelligent action than are generally found in the confirmation classes of the Episcopal Church.

With the diminished emphasis upon an experience of sin-consciousness as either a pre-requisite or sequent of church-relationship, it is not strange that another feature of the religious life of our time should be a considerably abated sense of the danger of men apart from personal experience of the Gospel's converting power.

Here again an alteration, not easy, indeed, to formulate or exactly to measure, brings the present into contrast with the past. Whether the reality of this change be tested by the utterances from the pulpit concerning the peril of unconverted hearers in the congregation, or by the more general arguments and appeals for sending the Gospel to those ignorant of it, the conclusion is the same. No such conviction as once prevailed, of the utter danger attending the condition of men apart from the Gospel, now dominates the exhortations of the pulpit or the appeals of the Missionary Boards. A glance through the sermons preached before our great Foreign Missionary societies, or even a recollection of addresses delivered in the hearing of such as have attended the anniversaries of these bodies for any considerable number of years, is conclusive on this point. No argument is here undertaken for or against the propriety or impropriety of this change, or the truth or falsity of any possible new conceptions of the real condition and prospects of men apart from a present experience of the Gospel's saving power. Still less is it attempted to set forth on what other possible points of religious truth the emphasis, lightened on that just spoken of, may now more strongly be placed, and, as some may say, may now rest with more than full compensation. It is only pointed out that, — however it may be justified or deplored — a change has taken place of such magnitude and extent as cannot possibly be overlooked. It is a change so great as to leave no room for wonder that our Universalist fellow-Christians frequently remark upon it, as implying a distinct approach on the part of Congregationalism generally to their principle of an expected salvation for all. Whether this implication is valid, or not, respecting Congregationalism as a whole, it is one which certainly has not only its apparent justification in the diminished sense of sin-danger which seems to characterize our pulpits generally, but its more explicit and positive confirmation, indeed, in the cases of some eminent leaders in our Congregational churches, whose Universalism is as pronounced as that of Murray himself, and whose standing as Congregational ministers is not at all thereby impaired.

Both the characteristic features of current religious conviction or sentiment to which reference has just been made are suited to awaken remembrance of another trait of the religious life of our time, to which they probably stand closely related, and out of which some may even go so far as to say that they have largely sprung. This is the very small amount of attention given in our time to systematic religious doctrine. The New England mind through a very large portion of our history has been strongly interested in theology. From the days in which the Massachusetts General Court set John Norton to answer William Pynchon's treatise on a view of the atonement which was substantially what is now, or has been till very lately, the generally accepted New England view, down through Willard and Edwards, and the great Old-Calvinist and Hopkinsian divines, to Bushnell and Park in a comparatively recent day, the study of religious doctrine has been a matter of characteristic employment. Times have been — these indeed were of long continuance — when nothing would so stir the blood of a New England congregation as a thoroughgoing discussion of some controverted point in dogmatic divinity. Amid the alarms of Indian wars, or the tumults of Revolutionary struggles, place and interest and absorbing attention could be found for the sharp distinctions of doctrinal analysis and the systematic statement of correlated truth.

It is needless to say how different it has been in the period now under immediate consideration. To call a sermon a "doctrinal sermon" is the shortest way in the popular apprehension to describe it as uninteresting and even unimportant. To suggest that a minister is inclined to doctrinal preaching is the surest method to prevent the consideration of his name by any parish committee in search of a pastor. And this popular distaste for systematic divinity is well indicated, also, in the subordinate place to which the subject is reduced in the curricula of theological seminaries designed for the express training of theologians. Once the central topic, to which all others were regarded as preparatory or supplemental, — systematic divinity has now to fight for its narrowed room, and to contend, sometimes with very partial success, for an equal standing place with many other subjects.

Yet it would not be right, in saying this, to convey the impression that preaching has probably either intellectually or spiritually degenerated. It has changed. But there is no evidence that, for the uses to which it has addressed itself and the altered requirements of altered conditions of religious life, it has deteriorated. It has become largely ethical where it was formerly dogmatic; practical, directive toward the prosecution of benevolent or Christian enterprise; expository of the requirements of personal, social, and public obligations; even, it may be believed, illuminative in many points of truer and higher conceptions of the divine character and of the mind of Christ toward men than formerly prevailed. How far it can travel the present road, especially in the treatment of political and so-called sociological applications of the Gospel, without suffering some loss of effectiveness in what now, as always, should be the main purpose of preaching — whatever the immediate subject-matter dealt with — may be an important question. But certainly in average skillfulness of method, and in intellectual ability and resource, the altered character of preaching has not been indicative of enfeeblement of mind or heart. They were not all Hookers, or Edwardses, or Bellamys, or Dwights, or Griffins, or Lyman Beechers who stood in the pulpit before our day.

The query just now suggested, however, as possibly arising, in view of the growing prominence of certain classes of subjects in pulpit discourse, which were formerly quite unknown there, leads to the more definite mention of a feature of the religious life of our time, of perhaps larger significance than any yet noticed in this lecture; namely, the changed conception which, in the past few years, has come into recognizable and apparently increasing acceptance, respecting the relationship of Christianity to society at large, or of the Church to the World.

Unquestionably the general conception entertained among our New England progenitors in the religious life was that of Christianity as an agency for individual rescue and salvation; and of the Church as the divinely appointed place of ingathering for souls brought home from a lost and ruined world. But just as plainly has there more recently risen in many minds the conception of Christianity as the savior of society, and of the Church as one instrumentality among others in an enterprise for the general redemption of humanity. The thought ranges over a wide scale of development in different entertainers of the comparatively new conception.

There are those who, while believing that the Gospel's hope lies in the regeneration of individual souls, recognize, nevertheless, the mighty influence of circumstances and environment in making this individual redemption more or less probable. They therefore look with interest and sympathy on all social endeavors to make as favorable as possible those outward conditions of life, which, if they do not assure the successful approach of religious motives to men, at least, it may be hoped, make that approach less difficult. To this end, they rejoice in whatever improves the physical and social conditions of a community. They look upon its schools and libraries and health boards as having a truly religious value; and especially are they interested in making the Church a kind of model of the regenerated society they anticipate, — a reformatory for the erring, a home for the homeless, a place of recreation for the tired, a restaurant for the hungry, as well as a worshiping place for the devout, — becoming thus an "institution" which is an epitome of a Christianized world.

Others, who have traveled farther in this direction, seem to fasten about all hope for the Gospel's greater progress, on a preliminary better adjustment of society; on better relationships between capital and labor; on a more equal division of property; on improved habits of living and increased facilities for education, holidays, and enjoyment. Some who are still called ministers of the Gospel, and who undoubtedly look upon themselves as the preachers of a more Gospel-like evangel than any hitherto proclaimed, unfold a system scarcely to be distinguished from the Socialism of any French or German doctrinaire. They denounce the Church, as it has been conceived of and administered hitherto, in its strenuous and dominating endeavor for the salvation of individual men out of a world lying in wickedness, as a positive hindrance to Christianity and a misrepresenter of the Gospel.

There is, as has been said, a considerable range of diversity in these positions. But the conception

THE CURRENT PERIOD.

of a relationship of the Gospel to society, hitherto insufficiently recognized, has unquestionably gotten a hold on men's minds, and to some extent has affected and modified the character of preaching in almost all pulpits. Whether it has so far affected it in any localities as to justify the remark of a very distinguished theological professor in one of the oldest Congregational seminaries, — that, judging from the sermons preached in his region, it appears that "the main business Christ came upon into this world for was to teach improved cooking and a better system of drainage," — is not here affirmed. But that the general conception to which the brilliant professor thus refers has its effect in altering the stress of the emphasis once put upon the individual bearings of Christianity; and, to some extent, in diminishing the intensity of the personal appeal, there can, I think, be no question. The single soul does not seem to weigh so much as it once did, when in former days it was so often set in significance over against a material world. The Church does not stand quite for what it did, when preachers of former days pointed to it as the Ark of safety from a Deluge close at hand. In this present time it is thought of by many rather as one of the various ships wherein men may be safely borne over the troubled waters of this earthly life. Membership in the communion of those who have been baptized into the name of the Sovereign, the Savior and the Sanctifier of men, does not amount to quite what it did formerly, now that the statement is so frequently made by pastors of Christian churches, that there are about as many true disciples outside as inside such fellowships; and that the command to acknowledge Christ before men has no very essential relation to a connection with the visible Church he has established.

Changes of mental attitude like these, to a considerable extent pervasive of New England religious thought, cannot be denied. It is not the design of these lectures to justify or oppose them, but only to call attention to them. As to how far they are an improvement in the religious life of the period, men will differ in opinion. But, as we have previously had occasion to note the fact that Universalist Christians seem to find a general approximation of all denominations to their characteristic view regarding another point of religious feeling of the time, so now it may not surprise us to learn, that Unitarian believers claim to discover in the tendency more immediately under consideration a significant approach to their thought of a redemption of man by education, moral improvement, betterment of situation and character, rather than by divine intervention through regenerating grace. An interesting confirmation of this claim of the approximation of Orthodox to Unitarian positions is the recent resumption of pulpit exchanges between two representative pastors of those long-time discriminated denominations in Boston. One of these pastors is reported in the public journals as saying that the event "means that the old quarrel of eighty years' standing is ended; and its causes were so long ago that only antiquarians remember them." If it be true that the great debate, from 1800 to 1820, concerning the person of Christ and the nature of his saving work for men, is a forgotten issue and an ended difference, it marks, indeed, an important epoch in New England religious history.

Another characteristic of the present period of religious affairs in New England, having a great, but as yet not altogether definable or determined effect on the religious life, is the changed attitude of the scholarly, and, to some extent, of the general, mind, respecting the nature and authority of Scripture. It is impossible not to recognize the fact of a wide-spread modification of that characteristic Reformation view of the Bible which regarded it as the direct and authoritative utterance, in all parts, of the divine mind and will. There was occasion in the first of these lectures to comment on the completeness of the acceptance of this view of Holy Writ by the founders of the New England churches, and the illustrations they gave of their convictions in legal enactments as well as in doctrinal discussions and homiletic exhortations. Undoubtedly a gradual and almost insensible modification of the full sweep of their practical claim that the Bible is everywhere, and in all points, equally inspired by the direct voice of the Holy Ghost, has long been in process. But it has been distinctly within the period which we are now con-

VIEWS OF SCRIPTURE. 185

sidering that the popular mind has awakened to questionings and doubts on this matter; as, also, it has been only within this period that these problems have been discussed in a really popular manner in pulpits, in familiar treatises, in newspapers, and in all common avenues of approach to the general thought of men. But, however recent the rise of such familiar discussions, there can be no question that they have already availed to put the Bible in a very different place from that which it has occupied historically in all the past of these New England generations. Instead of being the volume of ultimate and unquestioning appeal, at least on every moral and religious problem, the Bible is now, in the view of many devout and religious men among us — professors in our theological seminaries and occupants of our pulpits — a volume to be read with a critically discriminating eye, educated to discern what is and what is not authoritative and inspired in it. Its historic statements are to be tested as to their accuracy by evidences outside the pages of the Book itself before they can be fully depended on; and even the spiritual principles it seems to enunciate must be tried by their correspondence with what is true and right in experience, personal or collective, antecedent to their complete acceptance as universally established truth.

The compilation of Scripture through the hands of successive editorships of well-intentioned but fallible writers, — writers sometimes dominated by a dogmatic or ecclesiastical purpose stronger than a strictly historical or ethical one, — has introduced, it is affirmed, an element of uncertainty into the accuracy of a great part of Old Testament narrative, and into not a little of the New; and this even respecting alleged facts concerning the birth, the sayings, the miracles, the resurrection of our Lord. We are told, indeed, that the criterion of the critical consciousness, as well as the historic test, needs to be carefully employed respecting all of Scripture, in order to gain its true meaning, and to derive from this sifting its proper benefit. So much is this the case that a volume, recently written by the honored pastor of one of the oldest of Boston churches, and commended for its orthodoxy by the oldest Congregational religious newspaper, plainly sets forth the doctrine that it is Christ who is the verification of Scripture, and not Scripture which must be looked to as the verifier of Christ. This is a doctrine which, apparently, brings its reader again, more than two centuries and a half later, to that nearly equivalent statement which, in the teaching of Mrs. Anne Hutchinson, amazed the divines of that same city, and which there was occasion to notice in the first lecture, — "The due search and knowledge of the holy Scripture is not a safe and sure way of searching and finding Christ."

Find Christ first, and then test Scripture by Him, is the increasingly advocated modern view. But how to find Christ in the use of a Scripture which is not in itself authoritative, or which is authoritative only when adjudged to be so by some other test than its being Scripture, is a problem not so clear as one might wish it to be. The problem is stated nakedly and without any attempt to forecast its solution.

It is plain however, that the altered position which Scripture is to occupy under the changed conception which now seems to be on the incoming tide of acceptance, is already profoundly influencing, and is destined still more profoundly to influence, the religious life.

Many contend that the influence has already proved beneficial, and will become more and more so as the new method of looking at the Bible increasingly prevails, — that is, of looking at it as a literature; as a book containing, among a considerable mass of unimportant and inferior and even objectionable materials, some of the highest utterances of morals and religion ever made; as a volume which, when duly sifted from legend and editorial error, gives us a narrative of the most important events of human history in relation to God, and, above all, which tells us — attended, indeed, by some errors and exaggerations — of the life of the Divine Man, the most transcendent Personality who ever appeared among the children of men. Many whom we honor and admire aver that, as a matter of personal experience, the Bible was never before so interesting, instructive, or even so influential and authoritative, a book to them as when looked at through these modern lenses of historical and philological and spiritual criticism. It is difficult to deny allegations like these. The appeal to experience is one which always deserves a certain measure of respect.

It is an interesting question, however, among many which might be suggested, how far the new conception of the Bible will contribute to that source of Christian growth, which was once thought profitable and enjoyable in the experience of many former generations, and which was found in the reverent contemplation of extended portions of Scripture, and in their careful memorizing by the young. How many aged disciples have almost lived in Scripture story! What rich supplies of literally transcribed and ineffaceable utterances of what they deemed the words of God were engraved upon the tablets of recollection forever! What comfort they derived from these supplies in hours of physical labor, in times of bodily illness, in the watches of the sleepless night, and in the drawings-nigh of enfeeblement and of death! Will it be very much worth while, in the future, to record on those tablets what a critically revising new-editorship, supplementing the imperfect editorship of the original compilers, may conclude, with more or less of harmony, to be of abiding value? Or how can recollection well take hold of that which the coördinate faculties of historic, philological, and spiritual analysis are constantly exercised to discriminate and divide?

This whole matter of the changed and still

changing attitude of the time toward Scripture has important problems yet unsolved. That it is exerting, and is still further to exert, a powerful influence on the religious life, there can be no question. Whether this influence will be for good or ill is a question on which prophets prophesy variously, and the event can best decide.

Another thing, which the observer of the workings of the religious life of fifty or more years ago would find subject in our day to a very great change, is the form of endeavor very generally employed when a distinct effort for religious quickening is made in most communities. It has been already pointed out that, in the earlier of the great series of revivals which marked the close of the eighteenth and the beginning of the present century, very small use was made of itinerating evangelistic agencies in the promotion of the spiritually refreshing work; but that, as successive periods of religious awakening followed one another, the services, first of distinguished pastors, and then of a class of ministers more or less distinctly committed and segregated to this kind of work, came into general employment. The degenerating quality of these religious laborers, and the extravagances which attended many of their methods, caused the system itself to become the subject of very considerable controversy, and resulted in its comparative discredit and disuse.

This system, under somewhat altered conditions, has more recently experienced a revivification, and, it would appear, to a considerable extent, a reinstatement in public approval. These altered conditions, however, of the revived itinerancy are what give it its chief interest to a student of the religious life of to-day, and which invest the matter, also, with some degree of solicitude. Revivalism has come to be a profession, — one might almost say a trade. Bureaus for the furnishing of any applying community with an evangelistic worker are established, where lists of such available itinerators can be inspected; where their "records" are kept; where their peculiar adaptations to one or another class of people can be ascertained; where the probable cost of their enlistment for a revivalistic campaign can be estimated; and where, in some reported instances at least, the *per capita* expense of souls saved has been given.

It is certainly a somewhat striking fact, and one in itself calculated to arrest attention, if not to awaken alarm, that, in a period of time singularly destitute of those general movings on the spirits of men, which have been the occasions of the chief revivings of religious life in almost all our New England history hitherto, an agency so largely mechanical and bearing so many resemblances to the methods of commercial enterprise, should have so large acceptance. There were, indeed, great differences in the manifestations of revivalistic quickening characteristic of the earlier half of this century, — and differences largely owing to the quality of evangelistic agencies employed. Yet to one old enough to remember some of the powerful scenes of spiritual awakening of other revival days, or to those who read in New England annals the story of the revivings of years to which living memories do not extend, the present system of revivals to order, under the conduct of bureau-supplied evangelists, has its more than doubtful side. Can it be that the Christians of the New England churches need to go down to this sort of Egypt for help?

Our examination of the consequences of the Evangelical Reawakening concluded — at least that portion of it which referred to the state of religious feeling among communities considered as Evangelical and Orthodox, in distinction from those known as "Liberal" — with a few observations on what seemed to be the effect of the revival era, from 1790 to 1859, on the general feeling in reference to certain social practices. The altered position of the churches was noted — though it was remarked that there were exceptions to their uniformity of attitude — in reference to the convivial use of wine, to the theater, to dancing, and the playing of cards. That position was one of very general disapproval of these forms of social conduct. In a like spirit of faithfulness, to report rather than to judge the state of things in these communities to-day, it has to be said that the attitude now taken again shows a marked change. Certain forms of social enjoyment, now looked upon with allowance, were, indeed, frowned upon at all previous periods of our religious history. But there has been a manifest reversion, in some particulars, to views and conduct respecting these things, characteristic of times now more than a century gone. In almost all considerable towns the theater is a part of the generally adopted appliances of public amusement, and is largely attended by members of evangelical churches, especially Episcopal and Congregational churches. In these two denominations, certainly, the practice of card playing is common in all our larger communities; and participation in what the fathers used to call "mixed dancing" is equally so; while the social use of wine and spirits on wedding, and even on ordinary festive, occasions is not infrequent, and is plainly becoming more common.

But, while there has been this distinct alteration of standard as to what is regarded as allowable in Christian practice, there has been, also, as a feature of the period under present consideration, a large and increasing extension of what is regarded as obligatory in Christian activity. The sense of duty to do something, in some way, as Christians, has certainly been on the advance. It has already been mentioned that one of the first characteristics of the current era of religious affairs is its tendency to organization for combined effort. It should be added that organizations formed for Christian labor are not merely existent; they are employed. To a very great and commendable extent, Christian people use these agencies for the purposes for which they were devised. The members of our churches, in large measure, deem it obligatory on them to come into personal connection with one or more, or many, such instrumentalities of endeavor for others, for the Church, and for the Kingdom of God, putting into them time and money and individual effort. Especially is this the case with the younger portion of the membership of our churches, and in relation to forms of missionary and humanitarian endeavor almost numberless. Very few of those associated in the Christian fellowship — even of those more fashionable circles of society where conceptions of the allowableness of social practices alluded to in the preceding paragraph most strongly prevail — deem it a becoming thing not to identify themselves in considerable measure with some form or other of distinct effort for the good of men.

As a consequence of this fact, there is, unquestionably, at the present time a much greater variety and amount of Christian work — work which is the legitimate fruit of the Gospel in human hearts — in process and accomplishment every day among us than there ever was before. Energies at some former times pent up or paralyzed for want of channels of employment, or for want of intelligent understanding of objects to be pursued, are unlimbered and set in action on every side. Time once used in introspection and solitary thought is now, in very considerable degree at least, used in labor for others. Money is increasingly looked upon as an instrument whose best use is to do good with. A conception of stewardship for what is intrusted to men is, on the whole, growing in the Church, and is developing in the young. And if there is occasion to deprecate the existence of great fortunes gathered selfishly and used only for ostentatious, vulgar, and selfish ends, there are also frequent and splendid exhibitions of wealth used for the noblest and most Christian purposes; and of the best social positions and highest intellectual and moral advantages made tributary to the lowliest and most arduous Christian service.

It will, perhaps, be noticed, in concluding this survey of the passing period of religious story in the land planted by Pilgrims and Puritans, that no effort has been made, as one feature after another of it has been mentioned, to pronounce upon it as better or worse than what has gone before. For example, no verdict has been attempted upon the wisdom or unwisdom of the changed conceptions which are seen to be entertained in more recent days, respecting the lowered conditions of entrance into church relationship; upon the truth or falsity of the diminished sense of human guilt and danger; upon the growing outwardness of religious experience; upon the decay of interest in doctrinal truth; upon the altered attitude respecting amusements, or upon various other matters which have been mentioned. The neglect to attempt such a verdict has been intentional, yet not because, respecting some of these things, at least, a tolerably accurate and positive opinion could not easily be expressed. Such an opinion as to the relative worth of moral values in things as they are and things as they have sometimes been, it is doubtless the duty of a Christian pastor to have in the administration of his charge; it would be well for every Christian parent to have in the guidance of his household; it would be advantageous for every private Christian to have for his own benefit and direction. But the sufficing reason for declining, in a survey like the present, to attempt a point-to-point verdict on the changes which have taken place, is that things as they are cannot be looked upon as in any wise final. If anything is taught by a survey of the conditions of the religious life of New England for two hundred and seventy years, it is that every condition is but temporary. The course of religious affairs has not been regular, continuous, accumulative from generation to generation; but cyclic, often reversionary, progressive only by fits and starts, or, rather, it is at once more truthful and reverent to say, by the occasional, incalculable, sovereignly operative energies of the Spirit of God moving on the souls of men. So, there is every reason to believe, it will be in the future. And therefore, from the historical student's point of view, it is comparatively unimportant to decide, respecting any given moment of religious history, upon its value as compared with another moment a decade or a century before; for the lesson of the past teaches him that that earlier moment, in its more essential qualities, will, in all probability, return. Modified, indeed, as to its more exterior aspects and conditions by the necessary accumulations and inheritances of time, in its central and distinctive spiritual significance it will come again, and its dominating characteristics will again give quality to the period of its sway. Not but that, as has already been intimated, formal differences, and differences of proportion and degree, will always put contrasts between eras centrally most resemblant. History repeats itself, but does not repeat itself exactly.

For example, — to use perhaps the extremest illustration our survey can suggest, — should a revived sense of the inwardness of the religious life be awakened, as it is quite possible it may be awakened in individuals and communities, it would not be reasonable to expect it to take a form of such narrowness and intensity as it did oftentimes in the past. The manifold forms of modern activity have cultivated to so great an extent the outward side of piety, and have brought into existence so many established and necessary organizations and instrumentalities of outgoing endeavor, that they cannot but hold in check any too exclusive tendency to inwardness in religion. They must needs have a modifying effect even on the most introspectively inclined devotion.

But, with this qualification borne in mind, it is difficult to see why the characterizing traits of past

THE PRESENT NOT FINAL. 197

periods of religious life among us should not, under these suggestive limitations, repeat themselves.

Is interest in doctrinal religious truth now at a low ebb in our churches? What is to prevent its revival again? Not the unimportance of the subject certainly, nor the debilitation of the New England mind. Is the science of theology less inherently interesting than the science of sociology? Are the laws and operations of that Divine Word which pierces "to the dividing asunder of soul and spirit, and is a discerner of the thoughts and intents of the heart," less necessary to be understood or less momentous in results than the operations of the Roentgen rays which discover a buckshot lodged in the muscles of one's arm? Only the preoccupation and diversion of men's minds — through causes many of which can easily be discerned — prevent a return to sincere and pervasive inquiry into theological truth, — a return which is at no time impossible, and of which there are even now not wanting indicative signs. Such a return, no doubt, there will be. Again, under altered forms suited to an altered time, and in phrases harmonious with the altered form, will New England congregations follow the unfoldings of God's great plan of providence and grace as interestedly as they ever did in the days of Edwards or Bellamy or Dwight.

Are we told that the conception of the relationship of salvation to society has about crowded out the sense of its relation to the individual, and that the feeling of personal guilt and loss has about vanished from experience? Those personal convictions will awake, will arise, will thrill and control the spirits of men in large measure as they did aforetime. Over as hushed and awed assemblies as ever listened to a sinner's cry will sound again the ancient call, the call of every soul comprehending its own necessity, "Men and brethren, what must I do to be saved?"

Have those mysterious breathings of spiritual energy, coming no one can tell whence, and going no one can tell whither, which have in the past of our history been the chief agent in the conversion of men and the upbuilding of the Church, now for a considerable time been largely absent from us? They will return. God will revive His work. Again the still, small voice, mightier than the whirlwind or the fire, will sound athwart the chatterings of human frivolity and the bickerings of politics and of trade; and men will fall on their knees, in awe of an almost visible God, and in the trembling conviction that the one great necessity of a sinful soul is to become a subject of His forgiving and transforming grace.

The proper attitude of a student of religious history is patience and expectancy. Let him watch. Let him wait. Let him labor as best he can in his little day.

"God fulfils himself in many ways."

And He is surely bringing forward, though in ways which oftentimes seem to His anxious and toiling children to be blind, circuitous, and incomprehensible, that —

> "one far-off divine event,
> To which the whole creation moves," —

the Kingdom of the Lord and of His Christ.

INDEX.

ABBOT, Archbishop George, 16.
Ability, natural and moral, 132, 138.
Activities, Christian, 170, 171, 192–194.
Adams, Brooks, 79.
Allen, Rev. James, 159.
American Board, 155.
Andover Seminary, 155, 160.
Audros, Sir Edmund, 53.
Anthology, the Monthly, 160, 161.
Anxious Seat, 148.
Arminianism, 14, 122, 123.
Articles, the Thirty-nine, 14, 17; the Lambeth, 15.
Awakening, see Revival.

BANGOR Seminary, 155.
Baptist Missionary Union, 155.
Baptists, intolerance toward, 58, 59; church in Boston, 59; missions, 153–155; theological seminary, 155.
Beecher, Rev. Lyman, 148, 163, 179.
Belcher, Gov. Jonathan, 88.
Bellamy, Rev. Joseph, of Bethlehem, Conn., as a preacher, 103; theologian, 110, 130; opposes Half-way Covenant, 120.
Benevolence, doctrine of Edwardeans, 131, 132, 139, 141, 144.
Berkshire Divinity, 133.
Bible Societies, 154.
Board, American, see American Board.
Bradford, Major John, 51.
Bradford, Lieut. Samuel, 51.
Bradford, Gov. William, 41, 51.
Bradford, Major William, 51.
Bradstreet, Gov. Simon, 50.
Brattle Street Church, 78, 79, 160.
Brewster, Elder William, 163.
Briant, Rev. Lemuel, of Quincy, Mass., 111, 127.
Brown, Rev. Clark, of Brimfield, Mass., 111, 125, 127.
Buckminster, Rev. Joseph S., 160.
Bulkley, Edward, *quoted*, 41.
Bulkley, Rev. Peter, 38.
Bundling, 75–77.
Burchard, Rev. Jedediah, 147.

INDEX.

Bushnell, Rev. Horace, 177.
Butler, Bishop Joseph, 152.

CALVINISM, in England under Elizabeth, 14; influences founders of N. E., 15–17.
Calvinists, "Consistent," 134.
Card-playing, 191, 192.
Cartwright, Thomas, influence on founders of N. E., 15.
Channing, Rev. William E., 111, 160, 162.
Charles I., tries to check Calvinistic preaching, 17.
Chauncy, Rev. Charles, of Boston, on Great Awakening, 98, 99; theologian, 111, 125, 127.
Chautauqua Circle, 171.
Christian Endeavor Society, 170.
Church, present conceptions of, 180–183; "Institutional," 181.
Church-membership, conditions of, 29, 30, 61–63, 78–80, 173–175; how valued, 182, 183.
Clap, Pres. Thomas, of Yale, Old-Calvinist, 111, 125.
Codman, Rev. John, 161.
Cole, Nathan, account of Whitefield's preaching, 89–92.
Colman, Rev. Benjamin, 79.
Connecticut Evangelical Magazine, see Evangelical.
Connecticut General Association, missions, 153.
Connecticut Missionary Society, 153.
Consistent-Calvinists, see Calvinists.

Cooley, Rev. Timothy M., 147.
Cooper, Rev. William, 79, 85.
Cotton, Rev. John, of Boston, Calvinism of, 16; Hutchinson dispute, 38; versifier, 41; see also 159, 163.
Covenant, Half-Way, see Half-Way Covenant.
Currency, colonial experiments in, 55, 56.

DAMNATION, contentment in, see Hopkinsianism, and Willingness to be lost.
Dancing, 157, 158, 191, 192.
Danforth, Rev. Samuel, of Roxbury, Mass., quoted, 67–69.
Danforth, Rev. Samuel, of Taunton, Mass., quoted, 83, 84.
Danger of sinners, sense of, at present, 175–177.
Davenport, Rev. James, 95, 102.
Davenport, Rev. John, of New Haven and Boston, 38, 159.
Dedham Decision, 162.
Deerfield, assault on, 54.
Diphtheria, epidemics, 56.
Divine Sovereignty, see Sovereignty.
Dixwell, John, regicide, 53.
Doctrine, present lack of interest in, 177, 178; will revive, 197.
Drown, Rev. Samuel, Separatist, 117.
Dunster, Pres. Henry, 59.
Dwight, Pres. Timothy, theologian, 110, 125; modification of Edwardeanism, 150, 151.

Dyer, Mary, Quaker martyr, 57, 58.

EARTHQUAKES, 56, 84; religious results of, 84, 85.
Education, Puritan care for, 48, 49; decline in, 50, 51.
Edwardeanism, outlined, 130–133; in Evangelical Reawakening, 134, 136, 155, 160; its missionary spirit, 154, 155; see also 110.
Edwards, Rev. Jonathan, on "bundling," 76; revival in Northampton, 85, 86, 101; on extravagances of the Great Awakening, 94, 99; as a preacher, 103; on physical phenomena, 104, 105; on guilt of sin, 107, 108, 119; theologian, 110, 130; his hopes of the revival, 112, 124; opposes half-way covenant, 120; opposes Arminianism, 122; interest in missions, 154; see also 73, 150, 177.
Edwards, Rev. Jonathan, the younger, 36, 110.
Edwards, Mrs. Sarah, 104, 105; on willingness to be lost, 109, 143.
Edwards, Rev. Timothy, 73.
Emerson, Ralph Waldo, 159.
Emerson, Rev. William, quoted, 159.
Emmons, Rev. Nathanael, of Franklin, Mass., theologian, 110; on "means," 132, 133; on willingness to be lost, 143; revival measures, 148.

Episcopacy, introduced into N. E., 60; its view of church membership, 175.
Episcopius, Prof. Simon, 16.
Epworth League, 170.
Evangelical Magazine, Connecticut, founded, 153; quoted, 136–138, 142, 144, 145.
Evangelists, in Great Awakening, 95, 103; repressed, 111; in later revivals, 135, 147–149; in present period, 189–191.
Exhorters, 96, 103, 111, 123, 147.
Experience, narratives of spiritual, see Relations.
Externalism, see Outwardness.

FINNEY, Pres. Charles G., evangelistic labors, 147, 148; Hopkinsian preaching, 149.
Firmin, Giles, 27, 29.
Four days' meetings, 148.
Foxcroft, Rev. Thomas, 159.
GILLET, Rev. Alexander, quoted, 136.
Goffe, William, regicide, 53.
Gordon, Rev. George A., reference to a volume by, 186.
Graves, Rev. Increase, quoted, 137.
Griffin, Rev. Edward Dorr, on submission, 144, 145; preacher, 147, 179; at Boston, 161.
Guyse, Rev. John, 86.

HALF-WAY Covenant, nature and effects, 61-63 ; opposed, 113, 120, 125; abandoned, 156, 157, 174.
Hall, Rev. Gordon, *quoted*, 144.
Hallock, Rev. Jeremiah, *quoted*, 138, 145; revival preacher, 147.
Hart, Rev. William, of Saybrook, Conn., 111, 150, 151.
Hartford North Association, on revivalistic extravagances, 99; opposes Methodism, 122.
Hartford Seminary, formerly East Windsor, 155, 156.
Harvard College, 45, 48, 59; and Whitefield, 95, 100; Unitarian control, 159, 160.
Helplessness of man, doctrine of, 22-29, 64, 128, 132, 139.
Hemmenway, Rev. Moses, of Wells, Me., 111, 125, 150, 151; on use of "means," 129.
Higginson, Rev. Francis, 44.
Higginson, Rev. John, *quoted*, 44-46.
Hooker, Rev. Thomas, of Hartford, Conn., Calvinism of, 16; on human helplessness, 24; on willingness to be lost, 27-29, 108, 109, 143; on church-membership, 61; on guilt of sin, 106, 107 ; death, 32 ; books reprinted, 106.
Hopkins, Rev. Samuel, anticipated, 28; on willingness to be lost, 109; theological system, 110, 130-133; on "means," 132; controversies, 150, 151 ; influence, 152, 153; interest in missions, 155.
Hopkinsianism, 109; before Hopkins, 27-29; dominates Evangelical Reawakening, 134, 136, 155, 160 ; opposes New Haven views, 152 ; *see also* Willingness to be lost.
Hopkinsians, 133.
Hosmer, Rev. Stephen, election sermon, 74.
Hubbard, Rev. William, *quoted*, 45, 46.
Huntington, Rev. Joshua, 160.
Hutchinson, Mrs. Anne, on authority of Scripture, 37-39, 186.

INDIANS, evangelized, 33.
Intolerance, in early N. E., 57, 59, 66 ; toward itinerants and Separatists, 111, 115, 116.
Introspectiveness, 29, 30, 172, 196.

JAMES I., opposes Calvinistic preaching, 16.
Johnson, Edward, *cited*, 41.
Josselyn, John, *cited*, 41.

KELKE, Roger, English Puritan, 14.
King's Daughters, 170.
Kirk, Rev. Edward N., 147.
Knapp, Rev. Jacob, 147.

LAMBETH Articles, *see* Articles.

INDEX. 205

Land, desire to obtain, 51, 52.
Lee, Rev. Jesse, Methodist founder, 121.
Licentiousness, in early N. E., 75-77.
Luxury, 168.

MACAULAY, Lord, 49.
Massachusetts Missionary Magazine, 154, 160.
Massachusetts Missionary Society, 154.
Mather, Rev. Cotton, 28, 50.
Mather, Rev. Increase, 28, 163 ; *quoted*, 69, 70.
Mather, Rev. Moses, of Darien, Conn., 151.
Mather, Rev. Richard, of Dorchester, Mass., 16.
Mather, Rev. Samuel, *quoted*, 72, 80.
Mayhew, Rev. Experience, of Martha's Vineyard, 111.
Mayhew, Rev. Jonathan, of Boston, 111, 127.
"Means" of conversion, 64, 128, 129, 131-133, 141, 142, 150.
Methodism in N. E., 121-124 ; missions, 155.
Mills, Rev. Jedidiah, of Huntington, Conn., 103.
Mills, Rev. Samuel J., 145.
Ministry, education of, in early N. E., 50; converted or unconverted, 94, 99, 102.
Missionary Societies, 153-155.

NETTLETON, Rev. Asahel, 147, 148.

New-Divinity, *see* Edwardeanism.
New England Theology, *see* Edwardeanism.
New Haven Seminary, — Yale Divinity School, 155, 156.
New Haven Theology, 151, 152, 156.
Newton Theological Institution, 155.
Niles, Rev. Samuel, 119.
Norton, Rev. John, on Divine sovereignty, 18-20 ; his " Orthodox Evangelist " *quoted*, 19, 20, 23 ; on human helplessness, 23, 26; on willingness to be lost, 29 ; answers Pynchon, 37, 177 ; *also* 159.

OLD-CALVINISTS, 111, 155, 159, 160, 163, 177 ; views of, 128, 129; on sin, 131 ; revival of, 150, 151.
Organization, characteristic of present age, 170, 171 ; used, 192-194.
Outwardness, of religious life, 171-173.

PAINE, Rev. Elisha, 116.
Panoplist, The, 161.
Park, Prof. Edwards A., 177.
Park Street Church, 160, 161.
Parker, Rev. Theodore, 162.
Parsons, Rev. Jonathan, of Lyme, Conn., 103.
Pensions, 168, 169.
Perkins, William, English Puritan, 15, 105.

Peter, Rev. Hugh, *quoted*, 77.
Philip's War, 53, 84.
Phillips, Rev. Samuel, of Andover, Mass., 111, 150; on "means," 129.
Physical phenomena in revivals, 93, 94, 96-101, 103-105, 135.
Pilkington, Bishop James, 14.
Pilkington, Leonard, English Calvinist, 14.
Pomeroy, Rev. Benjamin, of Hebron, Conn., 103.
Porter, Rev. Eliphalet, 161.
Prayer, when sinful, 141, 142, 149, 150.
Preaching, present character of, 178-183.
Prince, Rev. Thomas, 85.
Punishments, Puritans not severe, 40.
Puritans, neither gloomy nor hard, 39-42.
Pynchon, William, volume on the atonement, 36, 37, 177.

QUAKERS, on authority of Scripture, 37, 39; persecuted, 57, 58.

RED CROSS Society, 170.
Reformation, character and results of English, 12, 13.
"Reforming Synod," see Synod.
"Relations" of experience, 29, 30, 78-80.
Responsibility, personal, 13.
Revivals, at Taunton in 1704, 83, 84; consequent on earthquake, 84, 85; in Northampton under Stoddard and Edwards, 84-86; elsewhere in 1734-36, 86. — The "Great Awakening" of 1740-42, 87-101; its physical phenomena, 93, 94, 96-101, 103-105; its evangelists and exhorters, 95, 96; its effect on preaching, 102, 103; on experience, 105-110; on doctrine, 110, 111; its results, 124, 125; political repression, 111; the "Separatists," 112-121. — Revival of 1797-1801, character, 134, 135; doctrines emphasized, 136-145; results, 146. — Revivals from 1805 to 1859, 146; modification in doctrine, 148-152; results, 153-158. — Will return, 198.
Robbins, Rev. Ammi, quoted, 138.
Robinson, Rev. John, Calvinism of, 16.
Robinson, William, Quaker martyr, 57, 58.
Rogers, Rev. John, of Dedham, Eng., 105.
Russell, Rev. William, election sermon, 74.

SALEM Bible Society, 155.
Salvation Army, 170.
Satan, belief in his agency, 31-33.
Schools, in early N. E., 48, 49.
Scripture, early translations of, 12; authority ascribed to in

INDEX.

early N. E., 33-39; criticism of, resented, 37-39; present changing attitude toward, 184-189.
Self-love, a motive in conversion, 151, 152, 156.
Separatism, story of, 112-121, 135.
Sewall, Rev. Joseph, 85.
Shepard, Rev. Samuel, *quoted*, 137.
Shepherd, Rev. Thomas, of Cambridge, Mass., Calvinism of, 16; on human helplessness, 23; few to be saved, 25; salvation difficult, 26; on willingness to be lost, 27, 28, 108, 143; "relations," 30; books by, reprinted, 106; *also* 131.
Simon, Rev. James, 119.
Sin, how presented by Hooker and by Edwards, 106-108; how viewed by Edwardeans, 131-133. — Sense of, in Evangelical Reawakening, 139-141; at present, 173-177; will revive, 198.
Slavery, 155, 165.
Smalley, Rev. John, of New Britain, Conn., 130.
Small-pox, 56.
Smith, Reuben, 158.
Social Usages, modified by Evangelical Reawakening, 157, 158; in modern period, 191, 192.
Sociology, 181, 182.
Solomon's Song, 34, 35.
Sovereignty of God, doctrine in early N. E., 18-22; in

Evangelical Reawakening, 130, 137-145.
Sparks, Rev. Jared, 162.
Stevenson, Marmaduke, Quaker martyr, 57, 58.
Stiles, Pres. Ezra, 155.
Stiles, Dr. H. R., 77.
Stoddard, Rev. Solomon, on Lord's Supper, 64, 86; revivals under, 84.
Stone, Rev. Samuel, verses on, 41.
Stoughton, Rev. and Lieut.-Gov. William, election sermon, 66, 67.
Strong, Rev. Nathan. as revival preacher, 147; as distiller, 157, 158.
Submission to divine will, 26-29, 108, 109, 131-133, 142-145.
Success, eagerness for, 167, 168.
Synod of 1637, 38; "Reforming," 47, 59.

TAPPAN, Prof. David, 160.
Taylor, Prof. Nathaniel W., views, 151, 152. 156.
Tennent, Rev. Gilbert. 95, 102, 105.
Theological Seminaries, 155, 156.
Throop, Rev. Benjamin, of Bozrah, Conn., 112.
Toleration, *see* Intolerance.
Torrey, Rev. Samuel, election sermon, 70, 71.
Tract Society, 154.
Tyndale, William, 12.

INDEX.

UNITARIANISM, antecedents of, 111, 112, 127; development of, 158-163; alleged approximation to, 183, 184.
Universalism, in Congregational churches, 176, 177.
University extension, 171.
"Unregenerate Doings," 141, 142, 150.

VANE, Sir Henry, 50.

WALLEY, Rev. Thomas, of Barnstable, Mass., election sermon, 67.
War, King Philip's, see Philip.
War of the Rebellion, 165-169.
Ward, Rev. Nathaniel, 27.
Ware, Prof. Henry, 111, 160.
Watts, Hannah, *quoted*, 119.
Watts, Rev. Isaac, 86.
Wealth in present period, 168, 193, 194.
Webb, Rev. John, 85.
Webster, Rev. Samuel, of Salisbury, Mass., 111, 127.
West, Rev. Stephen, of Stockbridge, Mass., 130, 151.
Whalley, Edward, regicide, 53.
Wheelock, Rev. Eleazar, of Lebanon, Conn., 103.
Whitefield, Rev. George, tour of N. E., 87, 88; his preaching, 89-92; its effects, 102, 103; his merits, 92, 93; his less attractive side, 93-95; opposition to, 100.

Whitgift, Archbishop John, 15, 16.
Whiting, Rev. Samuel, 84.
Whitman, Rev. Samuel, election sermon, 73.
Willard, Rev. Samuel, 71, 72, 177.
Williams, Rev. John, 54.
Williams, Rev. Solomon, 98.
Willingness to be lost, 27, 28, 108, 109, 142-145, 149.
Wilson, Rev. John, of Boston, 38.
Wine, convivial use of, 157, 158, 191, 192.
Winthrop, Gov. John, 50.
Winthrop, Mrs. Margaret, 40, 41.
Witchcraft, in early N. E., 32; in Old and New England, 40; in 1692-93, 54.
Wood, William, *cited*, 41.
Woman's Christian Temperance Union, 170.
Wycliffe, John, 12.

YALE College, Episcopacy invades, 60; Whitefield judges unfavorably, 95; testifies against him, 100; Edwardeanism of, 133; Pres. Dwight, 150; Prof. Taylor, 151, 152, 156; its Divinity School, 155, 156.
Young Men's Christian Association, 170.

www.ingramcontent.com/pod-product-compliance
Lightning Source LLC
Chambersburg PA
CBHW020904230426
43666CB00008B/1309